WITHDRAWN

DIALOGUES

DIALOGUES

Roman Jakobson
Krystyna Pomorska

The MIT Press
Cambridge, Massachusetts

Initial translation from the French by Christian Hubert

This book was set in Melior
by The MIT Press Computergraphics Department
and printed and bound by Halliday Lithograph
in the United States of America.

Library of Congress Cataloging in Publication Data

Jakobson, Roman, 1896–1982
  Dialogues.

  Translation of: R. Jakobson and K. Pomorska: Dialogues.
  Bibliography: p.
  1. Jakobson, Roman, 1896–1982. 2. Linguists—United
States—Interviews. I. Pomorska, Krystyna. II. Title.
P85.J3A3313   1983   410′.92′4   82–10055
ISBN 0–262–10026–6

CONTENTS

FOREWORD

The dialogues that make up this book explore the intellectual biography of Roman Jakobson, one of the seminal scholars of our century. The picture of Jakobson's thought and work that emerges from these pages is the result of a collaboration between Jakobson and Krystyna Pomorska, professor of Russian and Literature at MIT. Although the subject matter of the dialogues is Jakobson's career, the form in which the career is explored is largely due to Pomorska. In modern times it has been somewhat uncommon to deal with matters of serious scholarly and scientific concerns in the form of a dialogue, in part, no doubt, because the form is hard to control. On the evidence of this book Pomorska would appear to be a born master of this form. She knows when to press a point and when to give free rein to her subject, where further explanations are required and where additional elucidation would just add noise or tedium. Above all, her unparalleled knowledge of Jakobson's career, and of the intellectual and social background against which the career unfolded, enables her to focus the dialogues on the most pertinent issues and to elicit from her interlocutor informative answers that deeply penetrate the subject matter.

Jakobson's primary field of research is linguistics, the science of human language. In general linguistics, Jakobson's work of the 1920s and 1930s laid much of the foundation of structuralist phonology, the dominant trend of that time. The crowning achievement of this work was Jakobson's theory of distinctive features, which promulgated the idea that speech sounds (phonemes) are not atomic entities devoid of further analysis, but are rather complexes of phonetic properties (the distinctive features). This radical idea, though initially resisted by contemporary scholars, has now become the standard view, taught to students in the first few weeks of an introductory course, often without reference to its discoverer. Jakobson's second major contribution to general linguistics consisted in showing that the process of language acquisition by young children was in many important ways the mirror image of different stages of loss of language in patients with cerebral lesions. In his widely read study *Child Language, Aphasia and Phonological Universals* (1941, English translation 1968) Jakobson not only established previously unsuspected connections between acquisition and language loss, but also brought out important parallels between changes observed in language acquisition and loss and phonological change in languages that are genetically related as well as in those that are geographically contiguous.

Like most workers in linguistics, Jakobson has devoted much effort to the elucidation of particular points in the grammar of individual languages. He has written outstanding studies on languages as different as Gilyak (1957), a paleo-Siberian language spoken on the Sakhalin peninsula, and ancient Greek (1937). His major area of concentration, however, has been the Slavic languages, in particular, his native Russian, and Czech, the chief language of the country where Jakobson spent most of the years between the two World Wars. His analysis of the Russian verb (1948) not only solved a puzzle that had defeated generations of scholars, but also illustrated a new approach to such problems, which a decade later was to provide the model for generative phonology.

Outside of linguistics proper, Jakobson has made major contributions to studies of the history and culture of the

Slavic-speaking peoples, on the one hand, and to the study of literature and to literary criticism, on the other. In the former he has devoted a number of studies to the career of the ninth-century Thessalonian brothers, Ss. Cyril and Methodius, who firmly established Christianity among the Slavs and in the process established ideological positions on national self-determination that have continued to play a role in the political and cultural history of Eastern Europe to the present time.

During the Second World War, Jakobson organized in New York a project for the study of the *Igor Tale*, a twelfth-century Russian epic poem, which A. Mazon of the Collège de France had declared a seventeenth- or eighteenth-century forgery. The collective work on the *Igor Tale* published in 1948 not only fully established the authenticity of the poem, but also provided a completely new perspective on the history, the culture, and the literature of medieval Russia.

The study of form in literature has been a major interest of Jakobson's from the very beginning of his scientific career. In a number of studies going back to his monograph on Czech verse (1923), Jakobson has elucidated the role that different phonetic properties of the language play in verse. Perhaps of the greatest importance here have been his studies of meter. In particular, his discovery (1933) that the meter of the Serbian epic verse is based not on the regular distribution of stress, length, or syllabic structure, but on the presence or absence of word boundaries in specific positions in the verse. This was a novel suggestion at the time and provoked considerable resistance (and ridicule) from certain conservative scholars. Subsequent work, however, has fully vindicated Jakobson's hypothesis and has shown that word-boundary placement is basic not only to other Serbian verse forms but also to verse composed in other languages, in particular, in certain other Slavic and Baltic languages.

During the 1950s and 1960s Jakobson turned his attention to the role played in the structure of verse by morphological entities of language. In a series of studies now conveniently collected in the third volume of his *Selected Writings* (1981), Jakobson showed that such abstract elements as grammatical case, number, person, tense, and verbal aspect are distributed in particular poems in accordance with strict rules. These regularities are, therefore, every bit as important in our esthetic response to a poem as the more obvious formal devices of meter, rhyme, and assonance.

Jakobson must surely be counted among the most insightful literary critics of our time. He has written some of the best practical criticism published in the twentieth century, notably his appreciations of the Russian poets Khlebnikov, Majakovskij, and Pasternak, his studies of the Czech poet Mácha, as well as his commentaries on poems by Baudelaire, Poe, Shakespeare, Brecht, and others.

Last but not least, Jakobson is one of the great teachers of his generation. He is able to convey much new information to students as well as to inspire them to undertake projects that test the limits of their intellectual powers, to push themselves much harder than they had ever believed possible, and to succeed in researches that others had abandoned as too difficult. It is hardly surprising in view of this that during his two decades at Harvard Jakobson trained almost every major Slavicist active in the United States today.

In one of the dialogues Jakobson remarks that he grew up among painters. This fact, to my knowledge without parallel among major figures in literary studies and linguistics, is of fundamental importance for an understanding of Jakobson's intellectual makeup. The painters among whom Jakobson grew up were a rather extraordinary group: they constituted what has become known as the Russian avant-garde and included such artists as Filonov, Kandinsky, Larionov, Malevich, and Matjushin. The English critic John Berger.has remarked that in the few years before and after 1917 this group gave rise to "a movement in the Russian visual arts which, for its creativity, confidence, engagement in life and synthesizing power, has so far remained unique in the history of modern art" (*Art and Revolution*, New York, Pantheon Books, 1969, p. 29). This creativity, confidence, engagement in life and synthesizing power have remained constant factors in all of Jakobson's life and work. These traits enabled him to overcome the many disasters of our century and served to re-establish him each time he was forced by the history of our time to change his domicile and to start all over again. And it is these qualities that manifest themselves all through the pages that follow, as Jakobson discusses matters as disparate as the internal structure of phonemes and the literary politics of V. I. Lenin, the theories of the American philosopher C. S. Peirce, and the film *Last Year in Marienbad*. When asked to justify such ventures all across the map of human experience, Jakobson has responded that since language is central to all human endeavor, all this, and much more, is legitimately within the purview of his science, concluding with a paraphrase of the well-known words of the Latin poet Terence: "Linguista sum: linguistici nihil a me alienum puto."

Morris Halle

BY WAY OF PREFACE

The invitation to participate in the collection *Dialogues* and to sketch in this framework our personal experiences as explorers naturally elicited from both of us a deeply sympathetic response.

In language and in the science of language the presence of an interlocutor is of fundamental importance: the mastery of language is a dialogue, and the development of language is also a dialogue. The account of the relations between individual and collective contributions to the science of language and of its artistic transformation gains in productivity when submitted to discussion. Linguists have noted the existence of tribes which are familiar only with dialogic speech and for which monologues are totally alien. More precisely, these are tribes whose only speech outside of dialogues consists of ready-made ritualistic monologues. In our usual cognitive speech as well, monologues, much more than dialogues, are subject to ritualization. The temporal and transient shape of both creative speech and meditations on verbal creativity lends itself much more easily to critical debate than to individual report.

1 THE PATH TOWARD POETICS

KP   The foundations of your work in phonology have attracted
      special interest because of their links to poetry and to
      poetic language. You discuss this eloquently yet briefly
      in the "Retrospect" issued as an appendix to the first
      volume of your *Selected Writings*. This interest has re-
      cently increased following the appearance of three sig-
      nificant publications: the letters addressed to you by N. S.
      Trubetzkoy (N. S. *Trubetzkoy's Letters and Notes*, Mouton,
      1975), chapters of the autobiography of Kazimir Malevich
      in the volume of articles and material of the Russian
      avant-garde, with your postscript (Stockholm, 1976), and
      finally the *Ežegodnik rukopisnogo otdela Puškinskogo
      Doma* (*Annual report of the manuscript division of Puš-
      kinskij Dom*) of 1975, which contains the valuable cor-
      respondence between Malevich and members of the
      Russian avant-garde. These documents show the close
      connection between your research and the art of the
      avant-garde, while, it would seem to me, Trubetzkoy ap-
      proached the same set of scientific conclusions and results
      from a somewhat different direction, from ethnology and
      comparative linguistics. Aside from folklore, which nat-
      urally occupied an important position from the outset for
      him as an ethnologist, Trubetzkoy concerned himself with
      issues of verbal art only much later, when he applied to
      them the already elaborated methods of the "Formalists."
      Your own works on linguistics, on the other hand, pro-
      ceeded in parallel with your study of poetics. One is
      struck by the connection between the thoughts of the
      scholar and the artist. Comparing your *Novejšaja russkaja
      poèzija* (*Recent Russian Poetry*, 1921) with Malevich's
      reminiscences, and especially with his letters to Matju-
      shin, the reader is ready to believe that there is an in-

tentional exchange of views or at least a dialogue or common theme. Malevich intimately connects the questions of light and space in painting with the phenomenology of sound in verbal art. Some of his expressions are so similar to those of *Novejšaja russkaja poèzija* and even to those of your "Linguistics and Poetics" that they appear to have been borrowed from them; for example, when Malevich speaks of the "composition of verbal masses," or of the fact that until then "it was rhyme, not words, that was composed." Could you give us a more detailed and systematic account of these ties and coincidences?

RJ   Poetry was my first passion during the years I spent in high school at the Lazarev Institute of Oriental Languages. My very first attempts at writing verse were closely tied for me to the investigation of verbal art. I recall with some astonishment that at the age of nine or ten I was trying to represent the verses that I read, as well as my own feeble efforts at poetry, through peculiar metrical schemes that I would invent on the spot for the purpose.

KP   What year was this, approximately?

RJ   It was my first actual high school year in the Lazarev Institute, namely 1906–1907. Our instructors in Russian at the Institute were quite unusual individuals. In the lower classes we had Vladimir Vladimirovich Bogdanov, the well-known ethnographer and editor of the opulent *Ètnografičeskoe Obozrenie* (*Ethnographic Review*). He was also the private tutor of Nikolaj Sergeevich Trubetzkoy, who acknowledged his great debt to him and reported that "Bogdanov generally asked me to present him with outlines of compositions rather than finished texts because for him a rigorous plan of a composition was the

most essential thing." Trubetzkoy considered that this
precept later played an important role in his creative
work. Bogdanov was an exacting master and, as a teacher
of Russian grammar, utterly opposed to sterile cramming:
thus, for instance, he demanded of his students a precise
understanding of all meanings of the grammatical cases.
As a boy of ten, I was captivated by the task of compiling
my own long lists illustrating the different meanings of
each case, with or without a preposition, and compared
to every other case. The preparation of these notebooks
became an exciting game for me. I remembered this vividly, some thirty years later, when for the sixth volume
of the *Travaux du Cercle Linguistique de Prague* (1936)
I was writing a theoretical study of the general meanings
of the Russian cases where I systematically compared
them to their particular contextual meanings.

The lessons, or rather the lectures, of Nikolaj Ivanovich
Narskij were equally important for the beginnings of my
scientific career. The latter was an enthusiastic student
of such eminent representatives of the Moscow school
of literary studies as Nikolaj Tikhonravov (1832–1893),
who had a profound familiarity with Old Russian texts,
and of the folklorist Vsevolod Miller (1848–1913). I might
add that Miller was director of the Lazarev Institute during my first years of school. He left that establishment
during the first period of reaction following the revolutionary movement of 1905. Narskij himself was a pas-
sionate enthusiast of Russian literature, oral or written,
ancient or modern, and was able to inspire the same
enthusiasm in some of his students. It was he and Vsevolod Fedorovich Miller, by the weight of his authority,
who pushed me to collect and study Russian folklore.

From the outset, I was amazed that scholars were for the most part going off to distant corners of the country to look for works of folk poetry when a living tradition of folklore was to be found around Moscow and even within the city limits. So I began to collect Moscow legends and choral and ritual songs that had remained alive in the backyards of the city: the bits of rhyme and the interminable and unchanging songs hummed on the edges of Moscow, the popular beliefs and deeply rooted superstitions, the proverbs and formulas that embellished conversation, the counting rhymes and riddles of the children of Moscow. These first amateurish records prepared me for the real field work in folklore which I undertook during my first years at the University, along with two other, older students, Petr Grigor'jevich Bogatyrev (1893–1971), an ingenious ethnographer and my closest friend, and Nikolaj Feofanovich Jakovlev (1892–1974), who later turned from Russian oral tradition to the analysis of the phonemic and grammatical structure of language and in particular to the systematic study of the structure of the languages of the Northern Caucasus. It is worth noting that in our collective research and recording of popular works, we always insisted on working in an area close to the capital—in the districts of the old government of Moscow, that of Vereja, for example.

Although Narskij had furnished us with a wealth of material about the study of Russian literature and folklore as it was understood at the time, it was becoming ever more evident to me that the question of the very essence of literary art, as well as of the specific characteristics of its different epochs and schools, and its more prestigious representatives, remained unanswered. And it seemed ever clearer that these questions were closely linked to the verbal foundation of literary works, to their general character and individual properties. If I came rather easily to this fundamental conclusion, I must admit that the artistic life of the period gave me the basic suggestion, and for this I am deeply grateful. I remember distinctly that when I began to read newspapers toward the end of 1910, particularly their cultural sections, I found in the Moscow and St. Petersburg press reviews of the decade that had just passed. One of the common observations was, as they put it then, the end of Symbolism and the beginnings of the search for the new in literature and in art in general. So it was in the context of these "obituaries" that I first became acquainted and fascinated with the works of the younger generation of Russian Symbolists, Aleksandr Blok (1880–1921) and Andrej Belyj (1880–1934); whereas their elders, the Symbolist poets Valerij Brjusov (1873–1924) and Konstantin Bal'mont (1867–1942) left me cold. In the work of Blok and Belyj, one could already sense a new and very "immediate" attitude to the word.

Against this backdrop, the attempts to deal with poems and verse scientifically in Belyj's bulky volume *Simvolizm* (*Symbolism*), published in 1910, seemed perfectly natural. The idea of verse as the immediate object of analysis made an indelible mark on me. The articles in this volume were devoted to the study of a poem by Pushkin and to a review of the specific transformations of Russian iambic tetrameter in its 200-year history. The review prompted me to try my own hand at an analysis of this meter in the verse of the originator of modern verse forms, who had not been dealt with by Belyj: namely, V. K. Trediakovskij (1703–1769). A curious result of my schoolboy

efforts was the observation that both basic historical varieties of the Russian iambic tetrameter appear in rough
outline in Trediakovskij. It was only after him that the
period of demarcation and subsequent crystallization of
these forms took place.

I became even more intrigued by problems of poetic
structure through my studies of French poetry, in particular that of Stéphane Mallarmé. Mallarmé's verse and
his aphorisms on poetry unequivocally raised the most
essential questions of poetic structure and placed us
squarely against both the abstract and the concrete
problems of the relation between sound and meaning.
Mallarmé was included in my school curriculum. Our
professor of French, Henri Tastevin, was a dévoté of
French, as well as Russian, literature. He served for a
time as secretary to the editorial board of the Russian
Symbolist journal, *Zolotoe Runo* (*Golden Fleece*). Subsequently he was one of the first to popularize Italian
Futurism in Russian circles, and he also translated the
collection of Marinetti's manifestos into Russian. Because
I had a knowledge of French from childhood, Tastevin
proposed that I write compositions on Mallarmé's verse
instead of the usual French exercises. I chose his poem
"L'Azur" as my first subject. Then I became bold enough
to translate into Russian in verse and comment in detail
upon one of his most esoteric sonnets, "Une dentelle
s'abolit."

In 1912, Russian Futurist poetry, or more generally
speaking, avant-garde poetry, was beginning to take hold.
There appeared a whole series of neologistic discoveries
by the greatest Russian poet of our century, V. Khlebnikov
(1885–1922), whom I have always profoundly admired.

There also appeared the captivating manifestos and pro-
grams of the "Word as Such." This blossoming of modern
Russian poetry followed the remarkable developments
of modern painting, in particular French postimpres-
sionism and its crowning achievement, Cubism. Both
were widely disseminated in prewar Moscow through
reproductions and reviews in the press, and also by the
originals that held an important place in exhibitions and
in private galleries. I grew up among young painters, and
the fundamental questions of space, color, and the contours and texture of paintings were as familiar to me as
are the fundamental questions of the verbal mass in poetry
as compared to usual speech.

Beginning with the years just before the war, the figurative arts in Russia, concurrently with the experimental
theater in Moscow and St. Petersburg, with the innovative
projects in architecture, and, as we already mentioned,
with the seeking and striving in literature, had all acquired a truly worldwide significance. Such important
experiments as nonobjective abstract painting and
"supraconscious" (zaumnyj) verbal art, by respectively
cancelling the represented or designated object, strikingly
raised the problem of the nature and significance of the
elements that exercise a semantic function in spatial figures on the one hand, and in language on the other. These,
as it seemed, decisive issues in the search for a new art
and for a new conception of the elements of meaning
both in painting and in language were the basic reason
that brought the eager and curious adolescent into contact
with Kazimir Malevich (1878–1935), the tireless searcher
for new forms in painting, as well as with the penetrating
dissector of the word, Velimir Khlebnikov, and with his

---

enterprising and cunning partner, Aleksej Kruchenykh (1886–1968).

With Khlebnikov, I discussed the innermost laws of glossolalia (speaking in tongues) recorded in the eighteenth century among Russian religious sects, as well as the tissue of incomprehensible magical incantations, while Kruchenykh suggested nagging questions of possible correlations and junctures between the rational and the irrational in traditional and recent poetry. From the outset, we engaged in continuous correspondence and became true friends, which was perhaps not usually the case with him. Our friendship was marked by the joint publication in 1916 of a book of "supraconscious verse" (*Zaumnaja gniga*, with a punlike blend of *kniga* "book" and *gnida* "nit") which, when it recently reappeared on the Parisian antique market, had become an expensive bibliographical rarity. When I returned to Moscow in 1956, after an absence of thirty-six years, and upon my every trip thereafter, Kruchenykh came to see me at my hotel, and our old friendship continued and became even stronger. After his death, a clever Moscow woman who had known him wrote in a letter abroad: "He lived in his own world, and despite his practical, even mercenary spirit, he maintained only a distant relationship to the real world. Till the end, he retained his brilliant memory and utterly original mind which grappled with everything wondrous and strange. His common sense occasionally resembled madness. There were in him many elements of burlesque and parody that probably had remained with him from distant times, from his stage performances of 1913. He was a Futurist all his life—unfortunately only a few understand what this means." I believe that this reference to a Futurist frame of mind and manner is a deep insight.

It is curious that my closest ties were probably with the painters whom I came to know in the course of my discussions as a schoolboy—Pavel Filonov (1883–1941) and particularly Kazimir Malevich. The latter had broken with representational painting but was passionately striving to avoid self-sufficient ornamentality. Rather he endeavored to discover meaningful elements directly in pictorial space. In both these areas his ideas paralleled my own. He was attracted by the fact that in my literary efforts and theoretical meditations I obstinately insisted on the avoidance of meaningful words in order to concentrate on the elementary components of the word, on the sounds of language in themselves, avoiding both any dubious analogy with music and any confusion between sounds and writing. Such an approach, which pleased Malevich, continued to hold his attention after it brought us together in 1913. It was at this time that we hit upon the plan of going to Paris in the summer of 1914 to mount an exhibition of his most recent works. My role would have consisted of giving an oral commentary on his work in French and of trying to disseminate in the West our ideas on the outlooks of this new art. It was the war, more than anything else, that kept us from realizing this ambitious plan.

In 1914 I entered the historico-philological faculty at the University of Moscow. At the office of the faculty, I was presented with a list of its different departments, and without even reading it to the end, I immediately registered in the language section of the Department of Slavic and Russian, because the analysis of language seemed to me to be as essential to the understanding of literature as it was to that of folklore and culture in general. The tradition of tying the study of language closely to that of literature was established at the University of Moscow in the eighteenth century, and was particularly cultivated by one of the greatest Slavicists of the last century, Fedor Ivanovich Buslaev (1818–1897), who had inherited from Romanticism the idea of the existence of an intimate link between linguistics and the study of literature in both its aspects, written and oral. The term *slovesnost'* (derived from *slovo* "the word"), which is still used in Russian to designate literature as an object of study and which solidly ties it to the "word," properly characterizes this tendency. The term is especially useful with respect to the oral tradition.

It should be pointed out that at the University of Moscow linguistics was one of the few subjects of instruction that were obligatory for all the students at the faculty. Here too was found the influence of one of the most important schools of linguistics of the period, the Moscow School, and its head, Filip Fedorovich Fortunatov (1848–1914), who had proclaimed as the primary object of linguistics the discovery of general laws of language. In addition to affirming the close links between linguistics and the study of literature, the faculty of the University of Moscow had insisted for a long time that there were indissoluble bonds between written literature and folklore, in both teaching and research, while, at the same time, the profound internal differences between these two domains of literature were also recognized.

The rigor of thought that the faculty of the University of Moscow inculcated in us (our colleagues in St. Petersburg used to call us the "armored Muscovites") guided my scientific work in the years that followed. Despite the sarcastic remarks of skeptics, it seemed imperative to me, in the modest role of an apprentice, to master in depth the rudiments of the sciences that I was studying, particularly those of historical linguistics and dialectology, as well as logic and psychology. At the same time, like all my fellow students, I conceived of the necessity of moving beyond the framework of traditional university study. It was in searching for new paths and new possibilities in linguistics, poetics, and particularly in metrics, with primary application to folklore, that we founded in March 1915 the Linguistic Circle of Moscow, dedicated to the pursuit of these aims. It was fully in character that the first papers of our circle were devoted to poetic language. This choice was influenced not only by the growing interest in poetics, but also by the fact that in the explication of new linguistic material we felt much less constrained by the received methodological models that still weighed heavily upon us. Finally, it was in poetics that the vital relations of the parts and the whole were most clearly apparent, and this stimulated us to think through and verify the teachings of Edmund Husserl (1859–1938) and of the Gestalt psychologists by applying their principles to this fundamental cycle of questions.

2 APPROACHES TO FOLKLORE

KP From the preceding there arises a new question about folklore that concerns the very foundation of folklore and the methods employed to collect it. Your description clearly indicates that you and your colleagues, in this domain as in others, proceeded along lines that were directly in contrast with academic tradition. According to "official" doctrine, folklore was a rather exotic phenomenon, as were the places where it and its carriers existed. In order to discover it, one had therefore to set out on an expedition as if it were the Golden Fleece. Such was the enduring legacy of the divorce in the St. Petersburg empire between the intelligentsia and the "people," who had come to be considered a world apart from the culture of the upper classes. The projects of your group, on the other hand, already embodied a modern attitude. You could find folklore in your neighborhood; you could discern mythological elements where others did not even suspect they existed. Modern anthropology holds the same point of view and detects the conscious and unconscious mythic elements of a people in all manifestations of its life. The same tendency is to be seen in the attempts to reconstruct such elements that are being undertaken in our time by a group of Moscow scholars—the linguists and anthropologists V. V. Ivanov, V. N. Toporov, B. A. Uspensky, and others. The work of the contemporary Moscow School thus has something in common with your audacious seeking of that earlier time.

RJ The attitude of previous generations of scientists towards Russian folklore has been a complex one. In my time as a student the older generation had advanced a series of skeptical arguments. It questioned in particular the existence of a prehistorical oral tradition. Both in the West and in Russia, some scholars cast doubt on the original and intrinsic value of oral poetry. According to this line of thought, the latter was a series of echoes of the individual literary activities in the upper classes of a relatively recent past. Certain of these scholars tried to tie the emergence of all surviving works of Russian folk tradition with the Christianization of Russia and the institution of the Russian state, attributing the origins of folklore to the milieu around the court. There were even researchers who found this chronology unlikely and were ready to date the emergence of prototypes of the extant folklore texts, in particular the epic repertory, to the sixteenth century, and especially the time of Ivan the Terrible. It was believed that it would be easier to discover the best preserved and most rich vestiges of this poetic tradition that had supposedly filtered down to the lower classes in the remotest corners of the country, where living memories of the historical past could still be found since they had been least affected by the subsequent development and transformation of the country. Accordingly, the collection of folk poetry took place with the conviction that, the ideas of the Romantics notwithstanding, the mode of existence of folk poetry in its essence does not differ much from that created by individual writers. The variations that folk narrators would make on the texts of folklore were compared without reservation to the literary work of individual writers, and the recorders of folklore concentrated most of their attention on the personal role of its performers.

Step by step we had to overcome the principles and devices of our predecessors. As for the texts of folklore, we were ever more interested in the peculiarities of their structure. These texts were for us not so much fragmentary documents of the past as living works, thrilling the narrators as much as their public. It was becoming ever more evident that while the repertory might change with local conditions, Russian folklore was as fully alive in our immediate environment as in those far-off corners, and that the milieu in which it existed opposed its own folklore-based aesthetics and wisdom to our requirements and views. The independence of the folklore milieu struck us at every step of our research. In this sense, the study of a nearby region often provided more obvious, concrete, and richer experience than that of remote corners. The very fact of coming into direct contact with the structure of folklore allowed us to see for ourselves that the oldest elements can be preserved and experienced directly even within a group where the conditions of life have evolved considerably from what they might still be in out-of-the-way areas of our country.

The analysis of works of folklore, their genres, and relations as a single entity opened our eyes to new problems, and in particular threw new light on immemorial mythical motifs. It is no accident that comparative mythology has progressed so much and that its theory has been so extensively developed in Russian and international research in recent years. The prehistoric antiquity of much that is hidden in these surviving elements becomes convincingly clear when one subjects the actions and magical beliefs of a contemporary folklore group to a systematic synchronic interpretation, as P. G. Bogatyrev did in the villages of the subcarpathian Ukraine. It then becomes obvious that the evidence of folklore has far deeper roots in the past and far broader extension in space than was formerly believed to be the case before mechanical precedures gave way to structural analysis of the diffusion of works of folklore. In the end the Romantic conception of folklore as a collective creation was rehabilitated in a somewhat peculiar way.

KP   You refer to the question of the collective censorship of folkloric works that you and Bogatyrev developed in an article in 1929, "O razmeževanii fol'kloristiki i literaturovedenija" ("On the delimitation of folklore and literary studies"). You attribute particular importance to such a censorship and consider it necessary for the very existence of the work of folklore. According to you, this process is analogous or even equivalent to that of the diffusion of individual neologisms: the latter can only enter into language, that is to say, become a part of the linguistic code, if the censorship of the speech community "admits" them. The question of collective censorship seems to be fundamental for your theory of folklore and its characteristic features. A number of further consequences then logically derive from this principle, which determines the special character of folklore in contradistinction to individual literary productions.

RJ   It is worth noting that this new idea was so different from the reigning opinions that even Bogatyrev suppressed the point on collective creation in the printer's proofs of the "Program for the Study of Folk Theater" that we prepared together in Moscow in 1919 and that he published in 1922. This was in fact the reason that I removed from the publication any mention of my participation in preparing this program. When, at the end of the 1920s, Bogatyrev and I worked out this question in a paper for

the *Festschrift* in honor of the Dutch linguist and folklorist
J. K. F. N. Schrijnen (1869–1938), we encountered on the
one hand enthusiastic support of our theses in a special
essay by Schrijnen and later in his book on Dutch folklore,
but, on the other hand, obstinate objections on the part
of Russian folklorists of the traditional tendency, in particular Boris Matveevich Sokolov (1889–1941). It has only
been in the past few years that our theses have been
translated into different languages and have become more
widely recognized in connection with the general development of linguistic and folkloristic theories. Yet even
today there are in the East and the West naive opponents
of collective creation who continue to assault the idea.

It is through the primary role of a kind of collective
creation in the formation and continuity of folklore that
it is finally possible to explain phenomena such as the
basic communality of features in the poetics of folklore
and especially the limited choice of plots that Vladimir
Jakovlevich Propp (1895–1970) outlined in his eminent
study on the morphology of the folktale. The possibility
of autogenesis of similar plots can at present be explained
by the idea of an all-round collective censorship. Similar
observations were made by A. P. Skaftymov (1880–1968)
on epic poetry, and by Bogatyrev in some of his early
work on the typology of popular narratives of anecdotal
character, which were discussed in the Linguistic Circle
of Moscow in 1919 when Bogatyrev gave a lucid report
on the classification of plots in folktales and anecdotes
concerning "fools." In this lecture Bogatyrev included in
a special, I believe his second, class those "fools" who
did perfectly sensible things, yet at inopportune moments:
who would cry out, for example, "to their everlasting

memory" at a wedding, or "long live" at a funeral. In this regard, Bogatyrev jokingly classified *Eugene Onegin* in the same category. Jointly with Bogatyrev, I outlined not only new questions of the interpretation of folklore but also new tasks for the collector of folklore. Bogatyrev insisted on the importance of collecting the superstitions that had currency among various professions. He published his observations on the superstitions professed by actors and sportsmen, and still planned to deal with the superstitions of the left- and right-wing members of the Czech parliament. Our project to study one of the most universal and viable oral genres—gossip—and more generally of rumors in the recounting of facts, remained unfulfilled. The experiences of the noted German folklorist of Prague, Albert Wesselski (1871–1939), clearly illustrate the ever-traditional nature of this genre. Upon hearing an account at a party in which one of the guests recounted an amusing incident he had witnessed on a Prague bus a few days before, Wesselski calmly remarked that the plot had made its first appearance in a particular work of Oriental antiquity and had subsequently passed to the West to acquire a certain popularity in the Latin texts of the Middle Ages. . . .

KP So this generation, separated from Romanticism by half a century, refused to recognize the intrinsic value of folklore and did not comprehend its particular character. This brings to mind an eloquent parallel: the "men of the sixties"—the Russian literary critics of realistic and sociological striving in the sixth decade of the past century—

did not understand the literature bearing the Romantic stamp. The critic Dmitrij Ivanovich Pisarev (1840–1868), for example, denied literary value to *Eugene Onegin*. There is a law of error in the history of science!

3 VERSE AND THE SOUNDS OF LANGUAGE

KP The connection between poetic language and phonological theory turns out to acquire ever new sides and aspects. The establishment of correlations between poetic material, even pictorial material, and the general questions of meaning is, notwithstanding its great importance, but one facet of this complex problem. The existence of a manifest hierarchy revealed by the very structure of verse is no less substantial. In Russia, verse has been an object of study for a long time, and it is in fact verse that served as a point of departure for the questions and debates on the nature of the linguistic material itself. The prosody of the Russian language was already an exciting object of preoccupation for Trediakovskij and Lomonosov, who were the first to reform Russian versification and to fix the norms of the Russian literary language in the eighteenth century. After extensive discussions on the subject during the nineteenth century, prosodic research was taken up by the symbolists, and by Andrej Belyj in particular, who, as you mentioned, gave impetus to your own work. Belyj made the next major step forward. He exposed the errors that had been committed in the treatment of verse and observed also that in addition to the ideal framework of oppositions, that is, the meter, there exists another less speculative and more empirical schema, that of "deviations" from meter. It became evident that this schema in turn constitutes a hierarchy. Should one seek there for some of the premises for your theory of binary oppositions? In high school you analyzed Trediakovskij's verse in accordance with Belyj's drafts. Prosodic features play an important role in the whole hierarchical system of verse, and these prosodic features are themselves organized into strictly binary oppositions, as you yourself showed in your book *O Česskom stixe preimuščestvenno v sopostavlenii s russkim* (*On Czech verse, especially as compared to Russian verse*, 1923).

In following the development of certain concepts of your work on poetics, I have felt that questions of phonology have been only timidly addressed in *Novejšaja russkaja poèzija* (*Recent Russian Poetry*, 1921). The entire book is written in terms of traditional phonetics. Only once did you observe in a footnote, "Euphony does not operate with sounds, but with phonemes. . . ." It is only two years later, in the book cited above (*O Česskom stixe . . .*) that one finds a real phonological analysis. Is one right in considering that the object of study itself—the metrical and prosodic composition of two contrasting systems, Czech verse and Russian verse—played a decisive role here? In such an enterprise, you could not avoid focusing on the strictly hierarchical binary structures, while your study of Khlebnikov (*Recent Russian Poetry*) was concentrated on the special qualities of Khlebnikov's poetic language. This is the reason that, in this book, primary attention is focused on paranomasia and parallelism, that is, on what Malevich referred to as "the composition of word masses."

RJ   As we have already indicated, the issue of the relation between the external, phonic side of language and its internal plane, the sphere of meaning, emerged with particular clarity in poetic language. This was one of the main stimuli that forced us to overcome the separation between the theory of the sounds of language and the analysis of meaning, which had been a typical feature of our university training. When I was editing with Khlebnikov his *Complete Works* in 1919—they were un-

fortunately not published at that time—I was trying to
capture the linguistic aspect of the different devices of
his verbal art. It is difficult to find a poet in whose work
the phonic structure is more closely linked, in both principle and creation, to the semantic plane. The phonic
analysis of Khlebnikov's poetic texture prompted use of
linguistic data about the sounds of speech. On the other
hand, the new light that the original work of this poet
shed on the sounds of language led me to question willy-
nilly the habitual conception of phonic material in linguistics and to subject it to a fundamental revision. Of
unexpected use here was the theory elaborated by
Baudouin de Courtenay (1845–1929) and his best disciples
which withstood the official doctrine and opened many
new possibilities despite all its unresolved contradictions.
The concept of the phoneme featuring an indissoluble
link between sound and meaning as developed by the
two most perceptive of Baudouin's Petersburg students,
Lev Vladimirovich Shcherba (1880–1944) and Evgenij
Dmitrievich Polivanov (1891–1938), played a guiding role
toward my study of the phonic means employed by
Khlebnikov's verse, and by poetic language in general.
Moreover, the application of this concept in poetic analysis led me inevitably to revise closely and develop the
theory of phonemes in their reciprocal relations, because,
as one must not overlook, any linguistic concept applied
to poetics automatically and inevitably puts into the
foreground the idea of reciprocal relations.

   The constant and stimulating discussions of the Moscow
Linguistic Circle constituted an even more important advance in our development from the old phonetics to the
new phonology. In 1920, immediately after these dis-

cussions in the Circle, I left Moscow for Prague, where I immediately became interested in questions of modern as well as medieval Czech verse. A comparative analysis of the clear analogies as well as the no less significant divergences between Russian and Czech versification led me to reflect upon the nature of these phenomena, and to seek the origin of the differences in the phonic, and especially the prosodic, structure of these two languages.

On my way to Prague, on the boat between Tallin and Stetin, I immersed myself in the verses of that marvelous Czech Romantic poet, Karel Hynek Mácha (1810–1836), and I asked a citizen of Prague who was aboard the same boat to read them aloud for me. I was struck by the profound unlikenesses in structure between iambic tetrameter in Russian and in Czech, and I was particularly astonished by the variety of rhythmical deviations from the metrical pattern that the Czech iamb permitted, but which in Russian were totally impossible. I decided to do some work on these questions of comparative metrics, and upon my arrival in Prague I spoke to the head of the department of Czech at the university, Emil Smetánka (1875–1949) about this discrepancy. He explained to me good-naturedly: "Don't bother with this issue; I'll explain the deviations for you. Our poets are simply such idlers [lit. *takoví lajdáci*] that they are too lazy to write according to the rules." This amusing explanation stimulated me all the more to study this problem, which was important with respect to language and to literature as well. It was thus that I began to prepare my book on Czech verse. This research clarified the connection between strong and weak positions in the line and certain linguistic prerequisites, as well as the no less important connection between the rhythmic phrasing of the line and the distribution of the boundaries of words and syntactic groups. Finally, the research brought out the role of rhythmic variations that is played in Czech versification by such significative elements as the contraposition of long and short vowels. All of this obliged me to work methodically at the systematization of the phonic elements of language. I attempted to work out these questions from the point of view of the specific task that every element fulfills in language.

In this way, the idea arose that it is necessary to treat the sounds of language scientifically by taking into account the relationship between sound and meaning. Here were the beginnings of a new linguistic discipline, of which only a few preliminary hints could be found in the scientific treatises of the time. It was in my book on Czech verse that it seemed for the first time appropriate to me to use the term "phonology" for this purpose, despite the many meanings that had been assigned to this term in older scholarship.

KP   What was the subsequent development of the phonological theory? Did it remain as tightly bound to the study of poetic language? What other linguistic phenomena proved particularly useful for the development of your theory? How was the principle of binary oppositions applied to this empirical material?

RJ   The difference between stressed/unstressed and long/short which I had to study in depth for my comparison of Czech and Russian verse directed my attention to the study of binary oppositions: on the one hand, to the common property of the opposites, for example, the vocalic quality of a vowel, and, on the other hand, to the mutually polar properties of such a relation—in this case the length or shortness of vowels. What was more, the analysis of these relations obliged me to abstract the binary opposition long/short from the qualitatively different vowels that were subject to a given opposition. In this way there arose, on the one hand, the idea of qualitatively distinct vowels, for example, the concept of the vowel *a* separate from any quantitative opposition; and, on the other hand, the idea of an abstract quantitative relationship between two poles of duration, that is, between length and shortness, separate from the common qualitative substratum of any pair of quantitative opposites. From the prosodic properties, where the possibility, or rather the necessity, of such an analysis was particularly clear and insistent, my investigations inevitably progressed to other pairs of sounds that lent themselves to a similar analysis: for example, the contrast of voicing vs. voicelessness that characterizes pairs of consonants such as *d–t, z–s, b–p, v–f,* etc. The analysis clearly showed the relative independence, both in the system of language and in linguistic thought, of such conjugate properties as voicedness and voicelessness, as well as of such higher-level units of the consonant system as *d/t* disregarding the presence or absence of voicing that serves to bifurcate these twofold units.

In the light of such considerations, my research on the phonological evolution of Russian and other Slavic languages led me toward the end of the twenties to recognize a special type of phonological relation which I have designated by the logical term *correlation*. This concept proved to be fruitful both for the description of sound

systems and for the explanation of their historical evolution as well. My first treatise on historical phonology,
*Remarques sur l'évolution phonologique du russe com-
parée à celle des autres langues slaves*, which appeared
as the second volume of the *Travaux du Cercle Linguistique de Prague*, was based chiefly on the analysis of
correlations. The book appeared in 1929, concurrent with
the *Travaux I*, which contained articles by different
members of the Circle on questions of phonology and
other problems of linguistic structure.

When we began to study phonic relations in light of
their significative functions, we defined the phoneme as
the minimal unit of language capable of discriminating
word meanings. At that stage of linguistics, the phoneme
was viewed as a sort of indivisible atom. In the meantime,
the analysis of phonological correlations had already
raised doubts about the indivisibility of the phoneme.
For example, if one takes the phoneme b, it is possible
to analyze it into a number of distinctive features; that
is, the characteristic of voicing vs. voicelessness on the
basis of the proportion $b{:}p = d{:}t$, or occlusivity vs. fri-
cativity by virtue of the proportion $b{:}v = p{:}f$, or again
the absence of nasality as opposed to its presence,
manifested in the proportion $b{:}m = d{:}n$.

The definition of the phoneme as a bundle of distinctive
features has imposed itself. Thus, the initial concept of
the phoneme as the ultimate unit of language yielded its
place to the simplest sense-discriminating units such as
sonority, nasality, etc. It was precisely this conclusion
that guided my definitions of the phoneme since the beginning of the thirties. Of course, the phoneme maintained
its importance, but it changed from a primary unit to a

derived one; that is to say into a combination of concurrent elements—just like the syllable, which is a derived unit in the temporal sequence of speech sounds. As a matter of fact, the new theoretical definition of the phoneme predated the discovery of the empirical data necessary to justify it. Although in the *Travaux* of the Prague Circle Trubetzkoy was already approaching the idea of decomposing the vocalic phonemes into constituent sense-discriminative elements, the analysis of consonants remained for a long time far behind.

4 THE ROLE OF CONSONANTS IN THE DISCOVERY OF PHONEMIC OPPOSITIONS

KP   If it was vowel patterns that were first to raise the essential
issue of phonology, one is once again tempted to link this
to the fundamental role played by vowels in verse. As
can clearly be seen in his correspondence with you, Trubetzkoy's first observations on the symmetry of sounds
also began with vowel patterns. How and when did your
research into the phonology of consonant patterns take
root? The question is all the more interesting as it suggests
a parallel with certain processes in the practice and theory
of poets themselves. In Russia as in the West, the avant-
garde poets were the first to bring up the question of the
role of consonants, whereas even Symbolists were almost
exclusively concerned with vowels. While Rimbaud
composed an "ode" to the vowels, D. Burliuk (1882–1967),
the Russian avant-garde experimenter in painting and
poetry, composed verses in which the "hero" was "the
consonant sound, that glowing male." Vladimir Majakovskij recommended having recourse in verse to the
"rudest" consonants of the Russian sound system. To
readers of the avant-garde manifestos, the thesis that
consonants are the basic raw material of poetry seemed
most daring. One should note that in your youth, you
wrote verse based on the strangest combinations of consonants. It would seem that for the scholar, too, conson-
antism is a difficult problem. Isn't this due to the fact
that it forms a more "latent" system in language than the
sound system, and that the texture of syllables assigns
the leading role to the vowels? One would like to know
if the history of other disciplines, such as acoustics or
the psychology of perception, contains parallels to these
phenomena in the development of phonology and poetics.

RJ   Once again, it was poetics that provided the initial impetus. I came to the conclusion in my work on Khlebnikov
that for the rhyme of Russian poetry nowadays "the consonants are of greater relevance than the vowels" and
that "this is a particular trait of modern euphony." Unlike
the Russian aesthetes of the last century, who recommended avoiding the "unharmonious" accumulation of
consonants in verse, we came to take special enjoyment
in these rocky and repetitive sequences. I can still remember the pleasure with which I read the lines by
Trediakovskij which his contemporaries condemned for
their awkwardness: for example, the line "V xvrastínnyx
skútavšis' kustáx . . . " ("Hidden in bushes of brush-
wood . . . ") from his *Oda vešnemu teplu* (*Ode to the
Warmth of Spring*).

After the eminent Czech poet and expert on verse
Jaroslav Durych (1886–1962) published an account of the
indigenous translation of my book on Czech verse (1925),
we began a correspondence devoted to questions of Czech
poetics. In his letter of May 5, 1926, Durych disconcerted
me with the question of where in the studies on phonetics
one could find a scientific classification of consonants
suitable for an analysis of verse. He allegedly had managed to find such information on vowels, whereas consonants were described as distributed altogether
mechanically. These were his words: "Even though, according to their physiology, consonants are classed into
a set of groups, this grouping is deprived of any significance for poetics." Durych was certain that consonants
"form a sort of musical scale," and he was looking in
vain for physical data "on the tonality inherent in each
consonant, whatever its place in a sequence." I was un-

happily forced to answer that there was as yet no rational classification of consonants proper. I held on to the letter from Durych, and the question he had raised remained for years one of the principal themes of my reflections and research.

In the summer of 1930, as I was preparing for the conference on phonology convoked by the Prague Linguistic Circle for the following December, I came to the conclusion that there had to exist an intrinsic analogy between the system of vowels and that of consonants, and that it was necessary to bring out the structural similarities and differences between these two fundamental classes of phonemes. Trubetzkoy's skeptical reply in his letter of August 17, 1930, did not affect my conviction that this must be the next objective in the comparative analysis of vowels and consonants.

Despite the fact that the motor analysis of the sounds of language was at that time much better developed than that of their acoustic aspect, it was clear to me from the outset that the auditory signal is the aim of our motor activity in speaking, and that the acoustic classification of the sounds of language, and of consonants in particular, must and can provide a more direct and precise answer to the question raised by Durych. It is especially in the interpretation of verse that the auditory aspect plays a decisive role.

The point of articulation used to be considered the basic criterion for specifying consonants. In our textbooks there were long ranks of discriminative points, beginning with bilabial, labiodental, and apical consonants and ending with palatals, velars, postvelars, pharyngeals, and laryngeals. The mutual relationships between all these articulatory series remained perfectly obscure: what are the primary properties that underlie all these distinctions? What are the general characteristics that, in the process of verbal communication, permit us to grasp and unmistakably and rapidly discriminate between each of these many consonants? In point of fact, it is precisely these general characteristics that allow consonants to play a substantial role in the texture of verse.

Judged by their point of articulation, labials and velars are far removed from each other; yet historical phonetics has shown that alternations between the two types of consonants occur readily in different languages. The Czech phonetician Antonín Frinta (1884–1975), unable to find an explanation for this fact, wrote half-jokingly: "Les extrémes se touchent." If we take this aphorism literally, the notorious linear sequence of points of articulation in the traditional consonant charts that begins at the front and ends at the back must then be rolled up into a circle. For example, the line of the four basic consonants of Czech, the labial *p*, the dental *t*, the palatal *t'*, and the velar *k*, is transformed into the following system:

$$p \qquad t$$
$$k \qquad t'$$

This necessarily raises two questions. In the first place, what is the acoustic property that unites *p* and *t* as opposed to the velar *k* and the palatal *t'* (represented in international phonetic transcription by *c*). In the second place, what is the property that unites *p* and *k* as opposed to *t* and *t'*? In psycho-acoustic terms, the definition of these two properties of sound perception suggested itself and found essential support in the sound analysis of poetry attempted by the noted phonetician and metrician Maurice Grammont (1866–1946).

Even though the perception of sounds is in the first place a psycho-acoustic phenomenon, the cited classification was repeatedly attacked as subjective and still lacking objective foundation. Meanwhile, in the interwar period, the psycho-acoustic analysis of speech sounds had already given basically satisfactory answers to the questions of the constitution of vowels, but it still lagged behind in the study of consonants. Nevertheless, the physical experiments of that time already allowed one to elicit the basic information on the physical nature of the chief differential properties of the consonantal system. Moreover, x-ray pictures of spoken sounds and their measurements made it possible to outline the major articulatory prerequisites of the most characteristic acoustic differences within the consonantal pattern.

In the dramatic conditions of the years 1937 and 1938, which foreshadowed the approaching tragedy, scholarly thought was unwittingly turning away from peripheral academic themes toward questions that seemed more important, more urgent for science. "For us the days of unhindered scientific research are numbered," my friend Petr Nikolaevich Savickij (1895–1968), the pioneer of structural geography, said to me. At the very beginning of 1938, when I was in Vienna after visiting Trubetzkoy, who was working intensely on his *Principles of Phonology*, I realized quite clearly that the concept of phonological system was unfortunately condemned to remain fragmentary as long as the principle underlying it, that of binary oppositions, had not been consistently carried through. There was probably never in my life such a feverish profusion of new thoughts and starts as in the beginning of 1938, when I succeeded, as I thought then and continue to think, in fully carrying out the decomposition of consonantal phonemes into their fundamental oppositions.

I immediately wanted to discuss with Trubetzkoy these exciting discoveries and the perspectives that I believed they opened up for phonology and general linguistic theory, so I dropped in on him in mid-February, 1938. For two days we passionately discussed the possibility of a new approach to consonants and to phonological oppositions in general. Trubetzkoy accepted some of my ideas but stubbornly questioned others, in particular tonality features of consonants. He felt that he was too far advanced in his book to reopen fundamental questions, particularly with regard to the classification of interphonemic relations that he had adopted. So he suggested that I publish my reply on the subject after the publication of his book. The sudden turn of events in 1938 deprived us of any possibility of further meetings and cruelly accelerated Trubetzkoy's illness. He died on the 18th of June, 1938.

KP   What directions did your work take after the death of Trubetzkoy? What were the repercussions of his demise on your scientific research, which until then, it would seem, proceeded through dialogues, with new problems and emerging directions being developed through discussions?

RJ   At the Third International Congress of Phonetic Sciences at Ghent in 1938, I read my "Observations on the Phonological Classification of Consonants" in which I summed up the results of my recent quest. It became particularly clear to me at that time that the formulation and elaboration of phonological questions had entered a new stage. It became possible to draw certain preliminary conclusions about the structure of the speech sound system. It came to light that the multiformity of phonemes in the innumerable languages of the world could be broken down into a restricted number of differential elements. These minimal characteristics could be ever more precisely defined at every phase, namely, at the psycho-acoustic, physico-acoustic, and articulatory levels. Points that had remained obscure at the outset, especially the correspondence between the linguistic role of each of these elements, their acoustic characteristics, and their articulatory preconditions, were being answered with increasing clarity and simplicity.

Through research it became apparent that it is not the points of articulation themselves but rather certain more synthetic manifestations of the activity of our speech apparatus that play a primary role in language and lend themselves to an ever more precise account. This in turn raised a set of new fundamental problems. It was now necessary to determine more precisely the motor basis of the differential elements on the one hand and their physico-acoustic and psycho-acoustic particularities on the other. But, most of all, a detailed inquiry had to be undertaken of the interconnection between these elements in order to determine their relative linguistic relevance. The points of departure and terms and concepts that I had used since my study of Czech verse in 1923, such as "phonological elements" and "phonological system," had to be reviewed and defined more precisely. In short, a great and significant amount of research remained to be done.

It was in this work that I most acutely felt the loss of Trubetzkoy. The long period of our collaboration, which, as noted, was of the nature of a continuing dialogue and discussion, had come to an end. From now on I would have to work alone and verify for myself future findings and subsequent hypotheses. In addition it became more apparent that my vivid collaboration with the Linguistic Circle of Prague—this, as it seemed, inexhaustible center for discussion—would soon come to an end, as would later the activities of the Circle itself. For me the years of homeless wandering from one country to another had begun.

5 THE EFFECTS OF INTERNATIONAL EXPERIENCE ON THE DEVELOPMENT OF LINGUISTIC THEORY

KP   These extended wanderings, despite the fact that they were imposed by the events of the war and took place under painful and dangerous circumstances, were extremely fruitful from a scientific point of view. For example, *Kindersprache, Aphasie und allgemeine Lautgesetze*, probably one of your most fundamental studies, was conceived in Denmark and Norway in 1939 and written down in Sweden in late 1940 and early 1941, at a time when events and circumstances seemed to have been least propitious for scientific work. Nor were your first years in America favorable for study. What influence did these frequent displacements and the different countries to which they led you—from Scandinavia to North America—have on your scientific thought?

RJ   It goes without saying that these abrupt changes more than once interfered with and modified my work projects. But I must admit that the succession of scientific environments, each with its own particular interests and local watchwords, allowed me to reformulate my own questions and to enlarge their scope. My months in Denmark, where I was in close collaboration with the Copenhagen Linguistic Circle with Viggo Brøndal (1887–1942) and Louis Hjelmslev (1899–1965), major figures in the history of the great Danish linguistic tradition, forced me to concentrate more deeply on the theoretical bases of phonology. On my own part, I questioned the attempts of the Copenhagen Linguistic Circle to remove phonic substance as an object of our science, and I insisted on the opposite necessity of detailed attention on the part of linguists to the relation between form and substance. At the same time, these discussions led me to carry to its logical conclusion the principle of relativism in phonological analysis. This principle had been enunciated already in the first two volumes of the *Travaux du Cercle Linguistique de Prague*, where the very idea was considered as a secondary notion, derived from the idea of phonological relations. But despite this premise, one can find here and there in the phonological works of the Prague orientation during the late 1920s and 1930s instances where phonological units are defined in absolute physiological or physical terms, rather than relational ones. I must admit that these debates on methodology in Copenhagen taught me to maintain a greater rigor in my definitions so as not to substitute illicitly absolute material terms for the strictly relative terms demanded by exact science.

It was no accident that I conceived the idea for my study of the phonic laws of child language in Denmark in 1939. This study was prepared for the Fifth International Congress of Linguists, which was to be held in Brussels in September but was subsequently suspended because of the Second World War. In response to the questions of my Danish listeners and interlocutors, I displayed in my paper two ideas that I had already laid down some ten or fifteen years earlier: the idea of a phonological typology of the languages of the world, and the idea of linguistic universals. As I emphasized in my 1939 report, the law of the superposition of values is a fundamental principle for the attainment of these targets.

The universality of hierarchical order, which manifests itself as much in the structure of sound systems as in the patterning of grammatical meanings throughout the world of languages, required for its verification an analysis of the most various languages, as well as an analysis of child language in its development. My stay in Denmark was marked by an attempt to unify questions of linguistic phylogeny with those of their ontogeny. I studied, therefore, the acquisition of the phonological system by children from different linguistic areas. The inquiry into the order of acquisition of phonological oppositions by the child revealed tendencies toward a number of typological observations on the languages of the world. The essential result of such a confrontation between linguistic development in the child and the structure of diverse ethnic languages was the discovery of the laws of implication which operate in the two spheres; that is to say, in both spheres the presence of an entity Y either implies or excludes the presence of an entity X in the same system.

As research advances, it is becoming ever clearer that such laws not only underlie the phonological system but also operate at the morphological and syntactic level. They serve to reveal the hierarchical nature of language in its different aspects and to determine the hierarchy of relations between language and other domains of culture. In his recent book *Signes et Symboles* (Paris, 1977), the astute Swedish linguist Bertil Malmberg correctly observed that the main point of my interests and scientific research was "a general principle of hierarchical structuration to which are subject not only all human languages but also all other systems of semiotic behavior as well."

I arrived in Oslo on September 1, 1939, the first day of the war. There I met Alf Sommerfelt (1892–1965) and joined him and a close-knit group of Norwegian linguists, all of them specialists in a great number of languages. Our deep interest in a multilingual comparison that would be based on a coherent set of methodological principles led us spontaneously to organize a collective work in comparative phonology. It seemed that here the questions of phonological geography that had so vividly interested workers of the Prague Circle during the thirties might find their concrete application. We knew that the diffusion of phonological phenomena extended far beyond the limits of a given language or family of languages, and that similarities were to be found between the phonological systems of neighboring peoples, even in cases of a complete absence of a common genetic ancestry of their languages. We thus decided to prepare a phonological atlas of the languages of the world, or at least of a part of the world. We started work on a phonological atlas of Europe, and different regions were assigned to specialists. We listened to and discussed their reports and finally made a first inventory of phenomena that should be represented on geographic maps. Tempting vistas began to open up. But the occupation of Norway put an end to this project, which, unfortunately, has never been taken up again and brought to a successful conclusion, in spite of the fact that an atlas of phonic and subsequently grammatical structures would no doubt give many a final answer to linguistic questions still open, as well as raise a number of new ones.

Our research work hand in hand with Norwegian friends traced the way to a high number of new objectives. The specialist in Semitic languages, Harris Birkeland (1904–1961), whose phonological observations on the prosodic evolution of ancient Hebrew led to some pertinent discoveries, planned in 1939 to work with me on the metrics of the lamentations of the biblical prophets in the light of phonological analysis. This work, which from the outset demonstrated the utility of phonological principles for the discovery of the laws of this system of versification, had to be abandoned because of the German invasion.

Through a strange concurrence of events I managed to reach Stockholm in May 1940. Once again circumstances determined the range of my phonological research. I owe it to the wealth of the medical libraries of Stockholm and to the personal help of the head of the psychiatric clinic in Uppsala, V. I. Jacobowsky, that I succeeded in carrying out a project I had cherished for many years, that of a linguistic study of aphasia. The mirror-image relationship between phonological losses in aphasia and the order of acquisition of distinctive oppositions by children was the subject matter of my book *Kindersprache, Aphasie und allgemeine Lautgesetze* (*Child Language, Aphasia, and Phonological Universals*), which I completed in 1941 in Sweden and in which my earlier guesses were further elaborated upon and verified on the basis of the material on aphasia that was utilized here for this purpose for the first time. These comparisons between language in its development and in its disruption prepared me for further exploration in the pathology of language.

Unlike the Norwegian and Danish linguists, the Swedish linguists of that time, with a few exceptions, were not interested in phonological analysis of linguistic structure, and, in my talks to the learned societies of Stockholm and Uppsala, I had to learn how to convey new ideas in a widely accessible form, avoiding as much as possible the use of new technical terms. This lesson proved useful to me later, and I am still grateful to my Swedish audiences for it. In Stockholm, I established close relations with two foreigners, specialists in Finno-Ugric languages, who held appointments in the local graduate school: Wolfgang Steinitz (1908–1967) and Janos Lotz (1913–1972). We would meet once a week to discuss pressing phonological questions. In these discussions all three of us were struck once again by the similarities of the problems in phonology and grammar exhibited in our examination of Slavic and French material, as well as Hungarian and the Siberian languages.

Once again, a phonological approach to questions of verse proved a necessity. Such an approach shed new light on the structural laws of poetry and especially on the problems of hierarchical relations between the diverse parts of a single whole. In addition, this work showed the need for the coordination and logical integration of elements pertaining to different levels in the structure of language. Lotz and I jointly prepared a set of statements enabling us to deduce all the metrical varieties of Mordvinian verse from a minimal number of strictly coordinated metrical laws. The Hungarian Institute in Stockholm published these theses in 1941, just before my departure for New York.

There I was invited to lecture at the *École Libre des Hautes Études*, which was organized in 1942 by a group of French and Belgian scholars who had been forced to leave their homelands by the German occupation. In my teaching I had to direct my attention primarily to the theoretical bases of my entire approach to language and to its sound structure. The first series of lectures that I gave at this school, published recently in French and English under the title *Six Lectures on Sound and Meaning*, focused on the principles governing the treatment of the relationship between the phonic shape of language and its semantic aspect. In my course, which was attended by New York students and by my French colleagues, as well as in my discussions with them, I took as my starting point the doctrine of Ferdinand de Saussure as it appears in a version of his *Course in General Linguistics*, left to us by his Swiss students and followers, Charles Bally (1865–1947) and Albert Sechehaye (1870–1946). The question at hand was to specify those aspects of de Saussure's teaching that were shared by my views and those that separated us from each other. First and foremost there proved to be a considerable break with the Genevan precepts even in their two fundamentals, namely the arbitrariness of the linguistic sign and the rigid insistence on the linearity of the verbal form. Our entire phonological analysis, with its systematization of minimal phonological elements, clearly illustrated this fact. It was perfectly logical to base an exposition of the new approach precisely on an explication of these essential divergencies.

One of the most fundamental and fruitful principles of Saussure was that of the "oppositions" upon which the entire system of a language is based. On this point, I followed Saussure with increasing insistence from the moment I became acquainted with his *Course*, which Sechehaye sent to me in 1920 shortly after my arrival in Prague. I had to explain to my listeners and colleagues at the School the nature of the development and modifications that I had brought to the idea of oppositions in general and its application to language in particular. As an elementary logical operation it was indispensable to delimit precisely the concept of opposition in relation to other kinds of differences. This characteristic of oppositions was stressed more than once by the theoreticians of the interwar period, particularly the Dutch phenomenologist Hendrik Pos (1898–1955) and the Russian dialectician Aleksej Fedorovich Losev, whose analysis of correlative terms keenly raised the issue of implication (*Muzyka kak predmet logiki*, Moscow, 1927; *Music as a Subject of Logic*).

The very idea of opposition implies that these terms must be binary, and this dichotomous relation is clearly evident in the system of language, both at the phonological and at the grammatical level. Saussure was profoundly correct when treating in his *Course* the presence and absence of nasality within the phoneme as a linguistic opposition, because the two properties that constitute the opposition are endowed with the ability to distinguish meanings. However, the attempts made in the early days of phonology to assign to the phoneme the role of a member of specific phonological oppositions were inexact. The question "To which phoneme is the Russian phoneme /b/ opposed?" does not have a reasonable answer. The phoneme /b/ naturally incorporates a series of phonological distinctions: that is, voicing as opposed to the voicelessness of the phoneme /p/, absence of nasalization in contrast to the nasality of the phomeme /m/, occlusion as distinct from the fricative character of the phoneme /v/, etc. The question of binary oppositions arises only when we shift our attention from phonemes to the lower phonological level, namely to differential elements or distinctive features. Voicing is of necessity contrasted with voicelessness and only with it; the presence and absence of nasality are necessarily and exclusively opposed to one another. In short, only on the level of these truly indivisible distinctive elements do we encounter actual binary oppositions that are subject to a consistent structural analysis. The mathematician Jacques Hada-mard (1865–1963), who had been attending my lectures on linguistics, observed that these ideas closely resembled problems and methods encountered in mathematics. Through conversations with another of my colleagues and listeners, Claude Lévi-Strauss (1908–), it became apparent that there was also a close tie between these linguistic questions and the themes and vistas of social anthropology.

During the forties, most of which I spent teaching at Columbia University, and during the following decade, when I worked at Harvard and the Massachusetts Institute of Technology, I came directly into contact with the out-look and interests of American scholars. Little by little I discovered that my way of thinking, which tended more towards phenomenology and was close to the experience of the Gestalt psychologists, differed fundamentally from the ideology of the behaviorists, who still exercised a profound influence on the thought of American scholars and of linguists in particular. It would be inaccurate, however, to regard these differences as a disagreement between American and European approaches to the the-ory of language. Edward Sapir (1884–1939) is an example of a researcher of genius who firmly avoided behaviorist devices, yet he is no less typical of American linguistics of the first third of this century and exerted a profound influence on the work of his students. Nevertheless, the American linguistics scene at mid-century was definitely dominated by the so-called Yale-Bloomfield school. This term is not particularly apt, for both Sapir and Leonard

Bloomfield (1887–1949) worked at Yale at the same time. What is more, Bloomfield himself assured me that no Bloomfield school existed. When I pointed out that a number of linguists identified themselves as Bloomfield-ians, he replied half in jest that those who applied that term to themselves obviously hadn't understood Bloom-field. This claim, albeit an exaggeration, did contain a measure of truth.

In his theoretical considerations of the bases of language and linguistics, Bloomfield had followed a tortuous path that led from the dogma of psychologist Wilhelm Wundt (1832–1920) to the speculations of Albert Paul Weiss (1879–1931), a peculiar behaviorist mystic. Weiss's hyp-notic influence on the anything but philosophical spirit of Bloomfield had the unfortunate result of narrowing the range of concrete questions addressed by Bloomfield in his work on different languages and on language in general. Nonetheless, one cannot help but admire the profound mastery and intuition for language that Bloom-field displays in his purely descriptive work. This di-vergence between Bloomfield's ideological foundation and his methodological procedures accounts for the am-biguity of his influence on such fundamental linguistic issues as the meaning of the word and the role of this meaning in the linguistic analysis of language. The in-consistencies that have been observed more than once in Bloomfield's approach to the problems of meaning are also responsible for the contradictory nature of his teach-ings on the phoneme, although here, too, his immediate and intuitive grasp of the material is evidenced in his phonological observations.

Unfortunately, it was precisely these attempts by Bloomfield to construct a scientific theory that would eschew the semantic aspect of language that grew after his death to have such an important and sterilizing influence. The history of linguistics has been marked more than once by the effects of ways of thinking that eclipse and even repress any opposing idea. A typical example is the long hegemony of the neo-grammarian doctrine in Germany. For a single school to monopolize the major issues of linguistics is also a particularly characteristic feature of American scholarship, and was clearly understood by that very talented proponent of the semantic approach to language, Benjamin Lee Whorf (1897–1941). He wrote to Trubetzkoy in the 1930s that it was easier for him to develop independent views on linguistics while working for an insurance company than to stay free when aspiring to an academic career.

The cornerstone for the formal development of our understanding of phonology was the relation between sound and meaning. In my American discussions I was obliged to insist in particular on issues of meaning, and to develop further the principles for applying these insights to phonology. The idea that Saussure had inherited from the ancient doctrine of the Stoics, namely, the conception of any linguistic sign at any level as the combination of two aspects of the sign, the *signans* and the *signatum*, had to be applied in a precise and consistent manner to all levels of linguistic analysis, taken separately or together. It was equally applicable to syntax, morphology, and the analysis of speech sounds. It was necessary to show that the opposition of the two aspects *signans* and *signatum* was itself a binary opposition and to extend the logical concept of binary oppositions to all grammatical and phonological phenomena. In so doing, it was particularly important to establish the differences between binary oppositions at the phonological level and those at the grammatical level. In the former, the opposition pertains to the sphere of signifying relationships, whereas in the latter it belongs entirely within the domain of the signified elements.

In treating this problem, it was important to deal in depth with a topic that I had indicated earlier in my European work, namely, the structural unity of the entire phonological system and the logical principle of binary oppositions underlying it and ensuring the unity of the system, as well as the optimal perceptibility of speech sounds. Attempts to consider binary oppositions as just one of the possible forms of purposeful differentiation revealed theoretical and empirical inadequacies bit by bit. At the same time, it was necessary to direct particular attention to studying and demonstrating the structural uniformity of the two sectors of the phonological system—the vowels and the consonants—while taking into account also their mutual opposition. In order to understand this combination of divergence and unity, it was necessary to determine as precisely as possible the underlying unity of the distinctive features of consonants and vowels, and at the same time to recognize the essential differences in structure and appearance of these properties, which are conditioned by the mutual diversity of consonants and vowels.

The differences of opinion as to the bases and aims of phonology meant that we had to familiarize ourselves with what had already been said about the role of sounds in language, and it was during my years in America that my attention became riveted on the first steps that had been taken toward that linguistic domain science now calls phonology. I was forced to conclude with astonishment that the philosophers of ancient Greece, particularly Plato and Aristotle, had clearly understood the minimal discriminating units of verbal significations, and that over the centuries scholars in India had engaged in reflections on this subject in a manner quite close to the tendencies of contemporary linguistic thought. A curious fact: the essential difference between the level of sounds and the level of words (what some scholars today call the "double articulation") was known to the scholastics of the Middle Ages under precisely the same name.

Most of my attention, however, was focused on the pioneers of phonology in nineteenth-century linguistics, especially the Polish linguists Jan Baudouin de Courtenay (1845–1929) and M. Kruszewski (1851–1887) who, according to Saussure's conviction, "were closer than anyone else to a theoretical insight into language, without leaving the domain of purely linguistic considerations." The no less perspicacious anticipations of their contemporaries, the Englishman Henry Sweet (1845–1912) and the Swiss Jost Winteler (1846–1929)—who apparently suggested the name of the principle of relativity to his student and boarder Albert Einstein—forced me to reflect on the internal and external factors that prevented the further development of phonology in the intellectual climate of the late nineteenth century. The persistence with which these precursors of phonology approached the concepts *invariant* and *variation* confirmed my idea that these conjoined concepts had to play their fundamental role in phonological analysis. The consistent application of these same criteria has been shown to be decisive for the analysis of the relations that hold between the phonological makeup of vowels and that of consonants.

At the beginning of the fifties, in connection with discussions on speech analysis at the Massachusetts Institute of Technology and the Psycho-Acoustic Laboratory at Harvard, I came in contact with Gunnar Fant, a young Swedish acoustician who had come to do research work at MIT. In the course of our conversations, it came to light that this penetrating scientist of rare experience had determined in 1949 the physico-acoustic essence of the difference between the velar k, on the one hand, and the labial p and the dental t, on the other, and the essence of this difference proved to coincide with the discrimination between the vowel a and the vowels u and i. Fant had published a brief Swedish report of his findings, but he worked at that time without contact with linguists and did not immediately evaluate the importance of his observation for the science of language.

Fant's remarkable discovery allowed me to complete the perceptual and articulatory definition of the difference in question common to both vowels and consonants by describing the acoustic correlate involved. We subsequently defined this correlate together as a concentration of energy in a central and relatively narrow region of the auditory spectrum, as opposed to the concentration of energy outside this region. This marked the beginning of my joint work on an exhaustive definition of the differential phonic means with Gunnar Fant and an observant young linguist from Harvard, Morris Halle, who happily combined broad linguistic erudition with a lively interest in acoustics. These intensive studies fascinated all three of us, and led to our publication in 1951 of a little treatise called *Preliminaries to Speech Analysis*, which was published in a limited edition by MIT and sent out by us in 1952 to various specialists for their criticism and further suggestions. We considered this survey to be a first landmark, to be verified and deepened later by further observation.

On rereading *Preliminaries* some thirty years later I can clearly detect its inadequacies, yet I also see its great positive attainments, which even today mark a step in the direction of further research. It will always be indispensable to operate with the essential principle of the indissoluble combination of the acoustic and the articulatory aspects of sound, although both kinds of characteristics will of course have to be formulated more precisely in the light of new experiments. When defining distinctive features in *Preliminaries* we attempted to present a true logical opposition, in which the two terms are naturally opposed to each other and the presence of one term automatically suggests its counterpart to the hearer.

One must be careful not to substitute a superficially empirical juxtaposition of two contiguous units for the logical opposition of two terms. Pseudo-phonological definitions in absolute terms must also be avoided: each opposition must be defined in strictly relative terms. The phonological analysis of distinctive features must not be reduced to a mechanical enumeration. By focusing more and more attention on the internal reciprocal ties between different oppositions, we become progressively more able to integrate the entire phonological system and thus to discover its conjugate underlying laws. Such is the program for present research, which I believe would lead to the fulfillment of the sound foundations on which our

Preliminaries was based, and to the overcoming of the unavoidable defects of our primer without corrupting its valid elements.

The idea of the correlation between invariants and variants common to all contemporary sciences must be consistently applied in the comparative phonology of the languages of the world. It goes without saying that proper attention must be paid to variations, without, however, losing sight of the universal invariants that underlie them. For instance, if we discover in the languages of the world that the tonality of consonants with a semantico-differential function displays a characteristic lowering, and then find that in some languages this reduction is due to labialization, that is to say, to a contraction of the anterior opening of the oral resonator, whereas in other languages it is the posterior pharyngeal opening that is narrowed, then comparative phonological analysis would have to take into account not only these two articulatory variants but also their invariant common essence, as defined on the articulatory, acoustic, and perceptual levels. It would be a methodological error to neglect either the invariant or the variant aspects of the analysis. It is only by consistently taking the invariants into account that we will be able to free ourselves from blind empiricism and create an adequate systematization of phonological structures instead of a superficial taxonomy. This is the only way to realize a relatively autonomous program of phonological analysis, which is the necessary condition for ever more vast and productive research on the relation between the phonic level and the grammatical level of language. The discovery of these relations is in turn one of the most important objectives for contemporary linguistics.

KP   Your new formulation of the question of the phoneme
      in light of binarism seems to mark a particularly important
      step in the scientific development of the humanities, for
      it deepens and considerably enlarges the question of the
      nature of systems. You have established a solid base for
      binarism, thereby raising the question of its biological
      underpinnings.

      Your criticism of Saussure, particularly of his concept
      of the sign as an arbitrary combination of sound and
      meaning, is quite similar to certain positions that you
      had earlier expressed in Moscow in your criticism of the
      early Formalists and their approach to meaning in poetic
      language. You reproached them for arbitrarily separating
      poetic language from practical language, often without
      taking into account the particular functional character
      of the latter. You returned to this question in your book
      on Czech verse, in which you took issue with a Russian
      article published in 1914 by Lev Petrovich Jakubinskij
      (1892–1945), "On the Accumulation of Identical Liquids
      in Ordinary and Poetic Language." You addressed your
      criticism to the members of OPOJAZ (*Obščestvo po izu-
      čeniju poètičeskogo jazyka*—the Petersburg "Society for
      the Study of Poetic Language") in general, for their al-
      together naturalistic conception of poetic language as a
      sort of datum "empirically" distinct from ordinary lan-
      guage. The struggle for a functional approach to language
      is fundamentally a defense of meaning, which in turn
      leads to a defense of value. The only one of your Russian
      contemporaries to share your position at that time was
      the late Mikhail Mikhajlovich Bakhtin (1895–1975), who
      has recently attracted considerable international attention
      after decades of total oblivion. Your criticisms of the epi-

gones and vulgarizers of Bloomfieldian doctrine in your lectures at Harvard and the Massachusetts Institute of Technology represent a consistent extension of this same tendency.

6 GENERAL ISSUES OF SOUNDS IN LANGUAGE

KP You devote a considerable portion of "Linguistics and Poetics" to yet another aspect of the sounds of language: their expressive and redundant features. Because these features are not part of the limited repertory of the sense-discriminating elements, some workers in the science of language seem to think that such ingredients are not worthy of linguistic analysis. For your part, you consider these features to be an important instrument of oral communication that is not to be reduced to its purely cognitive function. At the same time, the expressive (or emotive) and redundant features do not play a role in the rigorously systematic language of verse, where only the sense-discriminating features are taken into account. On the other hand you cite the example of emotive intonation, whose variations are capable of considerably modifying the information of the message as a whole. Can one also apply this to verse and say that emotive features play a role in the manner of implementation, namely the recitation of verse, while playing no part in its structure?

RJ In addition to the independent, sense-discriminating elements of language that are of primary importance in speech, several other types of features also play a role too important to be neglected. Once again we must rigorously demarcate the system of differential elements from the other phonic features; however, the latter also constitute an inalienable part of linguistic analysis whether they are redundant or expressive. One must forswear considering all these other traits naively as gross matter without linguistic value. Today, a sound of language is generally viewed in its entirety as an artificial linguistic device, created and existing especially for the purpose of language, which is and continues to be absent outside of language.

KP   In "Linguistics and Poetics" you also touch upon the symbolism of sounds as one of the capital questions of twentieth-century poetry and poetics. The Symbolists made this device almost the main content of poetry as such, in practice as well as in theory, by using it as the basis for their celebrated "sound correspondences." I recall that you once remarked in a lecture that the sound symbolism of the symbolist poets, often ridiculed in the past for its inconsistency and its untenable subjectivism, had again become of interest in light of new scientific research and psychophysiological experiments. The most recent work in this domain—that of Dora Vallier on the relation between the system of colors and the phonological system, for example—has shown that synaesthesia has become a fruitful area for interdisciplinary study.

RJ   The border of the past and of the present century witnessed a proliferation of conjecture and scholarly debate concerning the synaesthetic ties between the different sensory domains. Although the first reflections upon the various analogies such as that between the sounds of language and colors resulted in a number of subjective and debatable conclusions, today we can see possibilities for more systematic and objective research on this fascinating problem that lead one to believe in the existence of profound psychoneurological correspondences. The relations linking the distinctive oppositions of language and the systematics of colors in particular seem to open important and promising avenues for common research among physicists, anthropologists, psychologists, art historians, and linguists, provided these comparisons are founded on a consistent relativism. Even more instructive have been the results of experiments by linguists on sound symbolism, that is, the evident and direct association between the oppositions of speech sounds and the fundamental semantic oppositions of basic meaning, such as high/low, light/dark, sharp/blunt, joyous/sad, etc. It has turned out that phonic oppositions not only play a subordinate, mediating, conventionally-distinctive role with regard to grammatical entities of languages endowed with specific meaning, but that they also possess their own direct yet latent significance, which exerts considerable influence on the organization of the lexicon of language. What is more, these oppositions take on a clear and often dominant role in the different manifestations of the mythology of language, which attains its greatest force in poetic language.

If at the beginning of my research the problem of verse and its phonic constitution compelled me to develop my work on phonology, then the study of phonological oppositions many years later led me to clarify the latent essence of this content, on which a particularly bright light is shed by poetry, and which on the other hand gives us a new key for understanding poetry.

7 THE TIME FACTOR IN LANGUAGE AND IN LITERATURE

KP In one of your most recent theoretical works on the aims of the science of language among contemporary sciences—a short essay on the history of linguistics that appeared in 1972 in *Scientific American*—you referred briefly to the doctrine of the neo-grammarians, whose methodology was basically concerned only with the history of language. One of the achievements of Ferdinand de Saussure was to overcome these theories that had ruled for so long. But later, in his *Course in General Linguistics*, he in turn reduced the object of study of the system of language to only one of its aspects, namely its static synchrony. The two approaches—the historicism of the neo-grammarians and the static studies of Saussure—prove to be clearly one-sided. How can one surmount these flaws?

RJ Time as such has been and, it seems to me, remains the vital question of our period. In the Moscow journal *Iskusstvo* (*Art*), which came out for a few months in 1919, I wrote in an article devoted to Futurism: "The overcoming of statics, the expulsion of the absolute—here is the essential turn for the new era, the burning question of today." Our thoughts on time were directly inspired by the current discussions on the theory of relativity, with its rejection of time as an absolute and its coordination of the problems of time and space. With its percussive slogans and pictorial experiments, Futurism, too, exercised an influence. "Static perception is a fiction"— this was my reaction in this same article to the traditional efforts of painting to "decompose movement into a series of separate static elements."

  Such were the preconditions of my first contact with the theory of Saussure on the antinomy between status

and history, that is to say, between synchrony and
diachrony. My attention was immediately drawn to the
fact that synchrony, which is the ensemble of the phenomena of language existing in a community of speakers,
was equated by Saussure both terminologically and theo-
retically to a static state, and was contrasted by him to
another equivalence, that of dynamism and diachrony.
In criticizing this conception, I referred, by no means
accidentally, to the example of cinematographic perception. If a spectator is asked a question of synchronic order
(for example, "What do you see at this instant on the
movie screen?"), he will inevitably give a synchronic
answer, but not a static one, for at that instant he sees
horses running, a clown turning somersaults, a bandit hit
by bullets. In other words, these two effective oppositions,
synchrony/diachrony and static/dynamic, do not coincide in reality. Synchrony contains many a dynamic element, and it is necessary to take this into account when
using a synchronic approach.

If synchrony is dynamic, then diachrony, which is the
analysis and juxtaposition of different stages of a language
over an extended period of time, cannot and must not
be limited to the dynamics of the alterations of language
alone. One must take static elements into consideration
as well. The questions of what has changed and what
has remained constant in the French language over its
many centuries of development, or of what has not
changed in the different Indo-European languages during
the several thousand years of migration undergone by
the Indo-European tribes since the breakup of the proto-
language, merit deep and detailed study.

It is to Saussure's great credit that he placed primary
importance on the study of the system of language both

as a whole and in the relation of each of its composite parts. On the other hand, and here his theory demands significant revision, he attempted to suppress the tie between the system of a language and its modifications by considering the system as the exclusive domain of synchrony and assigning modifications to the sphere of diachrony alone. In actuality, as indicated in the different social sciences, the concepts of a system and its change are not only compatible but indissolubly tied. The attempts to equate change with diachrony profoundly contradict our entire linguistic experience.

In a linguistic community, it is inconceivable that modifications take place overnight, all at once. The beginning and end of each change are always recognized as such during a period of coexistence in the community. The point of departure and the end point may, however, be distributed in different ways. The older form may be characteristic of an older generation and the new one of a younger, or both forms may belong from the outset to two different styles of language, different subcodes of a single common code, in which case all members of the community have the competence to perceive and choose between the two variants. In other words, I repeat that coexistence and modification not only do not exclude each other, but are instead indissolubly linked.

Inasmuch as the start and the finish of a change simultaneously belong to the common code of a system of language, one must necessarily study not only the meaning of the static constituents of the system but also the meaning of the changes which are in *statu nascendi*. Here the Saussurian idea of changes that are blind and fortuitous from the point of view of the system loses ground.

Any modification takes place first at the synchronic level and is thus a part of the system, while only the *results* of the modifications are imparted to the diachronic dimension.

Saussure's ideology ruled out any compatibility between the two aspects of time, simultaneity and succession. As a result, dynamism was excluded from the study of the system and the *signans* was reduced to pure linearity, thus precluding any possibility of viewing the phoneme as a bundle of concurrent distinctive characteristics. Each of these mutually contradictory theses sacrificed one of the two dimensions of time, one by renouncing succession in time and the other by renouncing coexisting temporal elements. We insist on the discussion of these notorious attempts to impoverish the object of linguistic analysis, because the danger of such illegitimate reductionism has not yet been overcome.

It must be emphasized that the members of the speech community themselves contradict both of these restrictive measures by their behavior. The speech community tends to include the temporal axis among the linguistic factors which are directly conceived. For example, obsolete elements of a linguistic system are felt as archaisms and new elements as the latest in fashion. This phenomenon can be observed at the phonic, grammatical, and lexical levels of language. The temporal interpretation here should be understood as a metalinguistic fact. Convincing examples of conscious or unconscious behavior on the part of a speech community regarding distinctive features and their combination are provided by the productive processes of vowel harmony, which consists of extending the value of a feature of a given vowel to all the vowels in a word. The opposition of grave and acute vowels is treated in this way in the majority of Finno-Ugric and Turkic languages, as is the opposition of tense and lax vowels in certain African languages.

I have become increasingly convinced that a consistently synchronic conception of the process of linguistic change would permit one to avoid most of the errors and misunderstandings that arise in establishing and interpreting change in linguistic systems, especially sound systems. I became especially aware of this during the sixties when working on the apparently labyrinthine question of prosodic relations and their evolution during the period when Common Slavic was decomposing into diverse historic languages. The fact of the original co-existence of various stages of development lent explanation and direction to the seeming confusion, and enabled me to sketch the phonological change of the relations of quantity and accent in the Slavic languages at the dawn of their existence. The pivotal questions that had been raised by such experts as Christian Stang (1900–1977) and Jerzy Kuryłowicz (1895–1978) in their work on historical Slavic accentology therefore had to be reformulated in light of these two indissolubly linked criteria, simultaneity and succession in time.

KP   It is paradoxical how certain critics do not understand this new attitude towards history. In Bohemia, they accused your approach of being static in character, of giving a "purely immanent" analysis of linguistic and artistic phenomena, rather than a historical interpretation. This was, by the way, the first reproach addressed to the members of the OPOJAZ by the official literary establishment. It seemed to these critics that the idea of development was necessarily tied to a separation of the chain of events into "old" events, identified with movement, and current events, which for some reason were not supposed to contain any movement. By the same token they saw time as an object that could by analogy be divided into "dynamic time," that is, the past, and "static time," the present. It seems to me that this thinking reflects a lack of imagination about how time is experienced: for some reason the principle of a single time, constantly flowing and immutably dynamic, remained beyond the grasp of these critics. Hence we are confronted by events of the past and the present both in their totality and in their mutually determined aspect. This was pointed out by Tolstoj as the inconsistency of viewing "history" as consisting of facts in the stream of life that stand out because of their "dynamism" (that is, wars, the activities of "great men"), in contrast to the rest of life, the "ordinary" life that does not seem to develop. By the way, your introduction of the principle of relativity into your conception of linguistic change leads again to the idea of system in accordance with the binary principle: we cannot imagine the present without the past, nor the future without the present, etc.

The artists of the Russian avant-garde whom you were closest to—Malevich, Majakovskij, Khlebnikov, and others—were similarly fascinated by the problems of the dynamics of time. However, many of them (Majakovskij in particular) drew from the dialectics of time an absolute inference, one particularly characteristic of the avant-garde: they wanted to vanquish time, to overcome its immutable march. Like Kirillov in Dostoevskij's *The Devils*, Majakovskij believed that in the utopian future time would "fade from consciousness" and cease to be experienced by men.

From all that has been said here about the evolution of language, it is clear to what extent this set of problems served as the basis for the methodological principles of the literary studies linked to the OPOJAZ. In 1929 Tynjanov wrote an important study entitled "O literaturnoj èvoljucii" ("On evolution in literature"), in which he proceeds from the same assumptions in order to treat the question of change in literature and its dual synchronic and diachronic aspect. His article was a continuation of your jointly written declaration "Problemy izučenija literatury i jazyka" ("Problems in the study of literature and language"), which was published in *Novyj Lef (New Left Front)* in 1928. How did you come to write this statement?

RJ   It is worth noting that the problem of a historical approach was concentrated on with special attention by the scholarship at the end of the 1920s. I believed it appropriate that the questions involved in the application of this method to different spheres of human activity and creation should be formulated and presented for discussion in the form of a few succinct theses. In the fall of 1927 I prepared a text on the treatment of the phonological systems and their historical changes, with the intention of presenting it to the First International Congress of Linguists that was to take place in The Hague in April, 1928. After securing the written approval of my friends and close collaborators, the linguists N. S. Trubetzkoy and Sergej Josifovich Karcevskij (1884–1955), I sent my theses to the committee of the Congress. Both Trubetzkoy and I were amazed at the positive reaction of the Congress, and especially of W. Meyer-Lübke (1861–1936), the celebrated representative of the older generation of linguists who chaired the meeting that sympathetically discussed the principles we advanced. My collaborators and I were particularly delighted that our proposals immediately brought the international avant-garde of our science together as a group outside the official meeting halls of the Congress.

It was this success that inspired the manifesto "Problemy izučenija literatury i jazyka" (*Problems in the study of literature and language*), which I wrote at the end of the same year in close collaboration with Jurij Tynjanov (1894–1943), who was visiting me in Prague at that time. The short article was published in *Novyj Lef* upon Tynjanov's return to Leningrad and provoked a number of reactions from members of the OPOJAZ. The commentary that accompanies the new (1977) collection of Tynjanov's articles on the history of literature gives some details of this intense discussion. However, none of these reactions was published at the time, because the independent positions of the society became an object of official sanctions that soon led to the total suppression of this historic association.

In our manifesto we asserted that the immanent character of changes within literature and their close ties to the system of literary values necessarily implied a coordination between synchrony and diachrony in literature: the isolation of the notion of system from that of its transformation lost significance, since there does not and cannot exist an immobile system and, conversely, mobility inevitably presupposes system; evolution possesses a systematic character. This manifesto of ours remained sealed in silence in Russia for more than half a century. It was published only recently, in the collection of Tynjanov's writings mentioned above, long after it had often been quoted in the West, had been translated into a number of languages and had been the subject of an international debate. Our comparative study of language and of literature was important not only for insisting on the commonality of problems, but also for drawing attention to the mutual relation existing between literature (as well as language) and the different contiguous levels of the cultural context. And this relationship called for a wider structural elaboration, based on the new and fruitful semiotic concept of the "system of systems," in order to explain the link that united the different cultural levels without appeal to the confusing idea of a mechanistic sequence of cause and effect.

It is worth mentioning that, in October 1926, shortly after the founding of the Prague Linguistic Circle, when private reflections had given way to fraternal and lively debate, I wrote a long, worried letter to Trubetzkoy asking him to react to an idea that had come to fruition in my mind, the idea that linguistic changes were systematic and goal-oriented, and that the evolution of language shares its purposefulness with the development of other sociocultural systems. Although more than fifty years have elapsed since I wrote that letter, I can still vividly remember my anxiety as I waited for the reactions of that linguist and associate whom I admired above all others.

On December 22, Trubetzkoy answered me with one of his most significant messages: "I am in perfect agreement with your general considerations. Many elements in the history of language seem fortuitous, but history does not have the right to be satisfied with this explanation. The general outlines of the history of language, when one reflects upon them with a little attention and logic, never prove to be fortuitous. Consequently, the little details cannot be fortuitous either—their sense must simply be discovered. The rational character of the evolution of language stems directly from the fact that *language is a system*." Trubetzkoy went on to add: "If Saussure did not dare to draw the logical conclusion from his own thesis that *language is a system*, this was due to a great extent to the fact that such a conclusion would have contradicted the widely accepted notion of the history of language, and of history in general. For the only accepted sense of history is the notorious one of 'progress,' that queer concept which as a consequence reduces 'sense' to 'nonsense.' " Trubetzkoy agreed that

the other questions of the culture and people's lives also evolve according to an internal logic of their own and implement their own specific laws which have nothing in common with "progress." It is for this reason that ethnographers and anthropologists do not want to study these laws. . . . Our Formalists have finally started to study the internal laws of the history of literature, and their path will allow us to see the sense and internal logic of literary development. The evolutionary sciences have been so neglected methodologically that today the immediate task of each science is the regulation of its own methods. The moment for synthesis is not yet at hand. Nevertheless, a certain parallelism undeniably exists in the evolution of the different aspects of culture, and thus there must also exist certain laws which determine this parallelism.

KP   The commentaries that accompany the above-mentioned collection of Tynjanov's articles show the extensive reactions and passions your manifesto provoked in the ranks of the OPOJAZ at the time it was about to be dissolved. The commentators quote from the letters of one of the most active members of the OPOJAZ, Viktor Borisovich Shklovskij, in response to your call for a vital revision of the society's positions. Among those who "answered with emotion" were Boris Viktorovich Tomashevskij (1890–1957), the eminent mathematician and specialist on verse, and Sergej Ignat'evich Bernshtejn (1892–1970), the phonetician and student of poetry. Also mentioned are the reactions of Boris Isakovich Jarkho (1880–1942), who carried out statistical analyses of poetry, and Boris Mikhajlovich Eichenbaum (1886–1959), the celebrated historian and theoretician of literature, as well as E. D. Polivanov, the remarkable linguist and orientalist.

You said that questions of history were of general concern at the end of the 1920s. This remark is worth developing, as it of course concerns not only scholars but also artists and writers who had very close ties to science at that time. The first example that comes to my mind is the poet Boris Pasternak. It was precisely in the second half of the twenties that he turned to questions of history, which continued to interest him for the rest of his life. Trubetzkoy's remarks on the parallelism of the evolution of the different aspects of culture can just as well be applied to Pasternak's remarkable narrative "Vozdušnye puti" ("Aerial Paths"), written in the middle of the 1920s. Pasternak raises the question of the immanent forces in history that are conditioned by the mutual relations between the "particular" and the "general"; he rejects the sterile schema of causal ties into which some would like to force all the phenomena of life, while life inexorably overflows this schema as it would a narrow and inadequate container. In place of a causal chain of determined states, the poet advances the rule of confluence of circumstances and makes the historical and psychological principles coincide in their function: they disarm man equally in the face of the imposed and arbitrary schema of causality. As for the "historical" principle, Pasternak does not at all conceive of it as a progressive line, an ascending chain of causes and effects, but rather as a confluence of circumstances that takes place outside of man, on the aerial paths.

It would seem not to have been coincidental that you wrote at almost the same time a manifesto with P. G. Bogatyrev, "K probleme razmeževanija fol'kloristiki i literaturovedenija" ("On the problem of delimiting the studies of folklore and literature," 1928–1929), and a manifesto with Tynjanov on the study of literature. Popular oral poetry, acting as a link in the chain connecting phenomena subject to linguistic analysis and those that belong to literary studies, came to occupy its due place in your organizational and research activity.

RJ The presentation to the Linguistic Congress at The Hague and the articles "Problemy izučenija literatury i jazyka" ("Problems of the study of literature and language") and "K probleme razmeževanija fol'kloristiki i literaturovedenija" ("On the problem of delimiting the studies of folklore and literature") were followed by yet another declaration of principle prepared on my initiative at the end of the twenties. Bogatyrev and I wrote the last set of theses in 1929, parallel to the article "Fol'klor kak osobaja forma tvorčestva" ("Folklore as a special form of [artistic] creation"), and we published them in order to initiate discussion in the Polish ethnographic magazine

Lud słowiański (*The Slavic People*) of 1931. We questioned whether the "existence of works of folklore and that of works of literature" in fact represented two distinct concepts, and we asked whether the same was not consequently true of the heritage of folklore and the heritage of literature.

We contrasted the continuity of the folklore tradition with the discontinuities within the history of the system of literary values. The common notion of "eternal fellow travellers" was replaced by the idea of constant encounters and separations. The evolution of artistic tastes always resuscitates forgotten authors, who then become participants in the system of literary values of the given period along with its own poets and writers. This implied both a conception of time as discontinuous and the backwards march of time, which allows for a return to the classics or even for including in the modern repertory certain artistic values that originally went unrecognized; in short, their posthumous rehabilitation and revival. This entire set of literary problems sheds light on the character of the time axis in the development of language, in particular the difference between spoken and written language which made possible the renewed study and rehabilitation of older words.

KP   When you examine your own ideas on folklore and literature from the perspective of the years that have elapsed, you assign great importance to the question of values. One could even say that you have effected a certain reorientation by transposing (in a perfectly consistent manner, by the way) the idea of evolution into the idea of value. At the same time, Trubetzkoy also was concerned with analogous issues. In his collection of articles,

O russkom samopoznanii (*On Russian Self-Consciousness*), he attempted to define the social mechanism involved in the elaboration and exchange of values. Russian society before the Revolution consisted of two main strata, the upper and the lower. The role of determining and consolidating the hierarchy of values fell to the upper class; the lower class simply accepted it. There existed a certain "transfer" of these concepts of value between the upper and the lower stratum: a value which today is appreciated in the upper class will pass tomorrow into the lower class, later to return to the higher spheres duly transformed. Your declarations no doubt touch upon this transfer of values. The social mechanism for their elaboration as proposed by Trubetzkoy has clearly been superseded: there cannot be found today in either the East or the West a social structure that would lead to this form of creation of values and to such a mechanism for their movement. The situation is somewhat different and more complex, but the principle of a mechanism itself can still be of some use when applied to a new order of things.

When the issue of the successive stages of literature and returns to earlier stages (that is, temporary returns to the artistic values of another period) is raised, there reappears the question of the coexistence of linguistic phenomena from different stages in the history of a language, a question that was posed in relation to Saussure's theories as well. The time factor seems to take a remarkable number of forms in language. Couldn't one say that the essential creative force of language is manifest in precisely this diversity? As I recall, you emphasized more than once in your lectures that the essential power of language, and consequently the privilege of the speaker, lies in the fact that language is capable of transporting us across both time and space.

RJ   It would be difficult to find a domain in which the concepts of coexistence and succession are as intertwined as they are in the life of language and literature. A few clear examples will suffice. One of them refers to the perception of spoken language. Speech is transmitted at a rapid rate and demands that the auditor grasp a considerable part, if not all, of the elements that are needed for comprehension of the utterance. The listener becomes conscious of the words after the units of which they are composed have already been pronounced, and he understands the sentences after the words of which they are composed have already been uttered. In order for the utterance to be understood, attention to the flow of speech must be combined with moments of "simultaneous synthesis," as they were called a hundred years ago by the Russian neurologist and psychologist I. M. Sechenov (1829–1905) in his Èlementy mysli (Elements of Thought). This is the procedure that combines the elements that have escaped immediate perception with those that already belong to immediate memory. These elements are then combined into larger groupings: sounds into words, words into sentences, and sentences into utterances.

I would say that the role of short- and long-term memory constitutes one of the central problems of both general linguistics and the psychology of language, and much in this domain should be reconsidered and thought through more carefully, taking into account the entire range of consequences.

In one of his last novels, the poet Aragon quite appropriately mentioned the idea put forward by a few isolated linguists of the last century concerning the intermittence of recollecting and forgetting in the development of language, and the historical role of oblivion which is compensated by verbal creativeness.

Over the centuries, the science of language has more than once addressed the question of ellipsis which manifests itself at different verbal levels: sounds, syntax, and narration. It should be noted that for the most part these questions have been worked out only episodically and fragmentarily. A technique which today receives even less consideration is that of elliptical perception, by which the listener fills in (again on all linguistic levels) whatever has been omitted by him as speaker. We have also failed to appreciate properly the subjective attitude of the hearer who creatively fills in elliptic gaps. Here lies the heart of the issue of disambiguation, which has been the object of considerable debate for the past few years within the science of language.

From this angle one of the essential differences between spoken and written language can clearly be seen. The former has a purely temporal character, whereas the second connects time and space. While the sounds that we hear disappear, when we read we usually have immobile letters before us and the time of the written flow of words is reversible: we can read and re-read, and, what is more, we can be ahead of an event. Anticipation, which is subjective in the listener, becomes objective in the reader, who can read the end of a letter or novel before reading the earlier parts.

We have dwelt on the question of the mutual relation between phonemes and their constituent elements, that is, distinctive features, and this relation is essential for

the comprehension of the *signans*. Phonemes as a kind
of phonic cord (that is, bundles of concurrent distinctive
features) have analogs on the plane of the *signatum*. These
are bundles of simultaneous grammatical meanings ("cu-
mulations of signata," as they were called by Charles
Bally, Saussure's disciple and successor at Geneva). To
give an elementary example: the desinence *-o* of the Latin
amo simultaneously designates the person of the verb,
its number, and its tense. The transmission of such bundles of concurrent semantic elements by means of a single
segment within the flow of discourse is a characteristic
of the grammatical systems of the so-called synthetic languages. On the other hand, the agglutinative systems (for
example, the Turkic languages) furnish each suffix with
a single grammatical signification, and accordingly transform these factually coexisting meanings into a temporal
successsion of suffixes, each with its own value. The
capacity of two competing and essentially contrary factors,
namely simultaneous co-occurrence on the one hand and
temporal succession on the other, accounts for what is
perhaps the most typical manifestation of the idea of time
in the structure and the life of language.

A variety of conflicts arises between the two aspects
of time. There is on the one hand the time of the speech
event and on the other hand the time of the narrated
event. The clash of these two facets is particularly evident
in verbal art. Since discourse, and particularly artistic
discourse, is deployed in time, doubts have been expressed more than once over the centuries as to whether
it is possible to overcome in verbal art this fact of the
uninterrupted temporal flow, which opposes poetry to
the stasis of painting. The question was also raised of

whether painting is capable of showing movement and poetry—static description. Can one transmit through the means afforded to us by the flow of speech the image of a knight in armor sitting on his horse, or do the laws of language require that such a scene be presented as a narrative about the process of dressing the knight and saddling the horse? This was the argument of the German author Gotthold Ephraim Lessing (1729–1781), who proposed to replace, in poetic description, coexistence in space with succession in time. Lessing's younger fellow writer, Johann Gottfried Herder (1744—1803), answered with a defense of simultaneous phenomena that permit poetry to overcome the linear succession of the events it renders.

Tadeusz Zieliński (1859–1944), the Polish classical philologist, has shown that the impossibility of reconciling in language the constant progress of the narrative with the fact that a number of actions take place in different places at the same time was already realized in the epic tradition of the *Iliad*. In this story, the action of a given person is necessarily accompanied by disappearance and passive inaction on the part of all the other personages. By contrast, other poetic approaches make it possible to render several simultaneous actions dispersed in space. The time in a narrative can be reversed. The story may have recourse to retrospective reminiscences, or may simply start with the dénouement and then go back in time. Moreover, the storyteller may directly attribute an inverse order of events to the invented events themselves, as did the great Russian poet of our century, Velimir Khlebnikov. In a Khlebnikov tale the two heroes pass from the ends of their lives to the beginnings but continue to speak of the past and future in the normal and uninverted order of these times.

Finally, in the Easter play of the Middle Ages, which combines the mystery of the saints with a traditional farce of grotesque figures, the characters experience simultaneous existence in two temporal sets. On the one hand they participate in the unfolding of the events of the gospel story that preceded the Resurrection of Christ, while on the other hand they anticipate with pleasure the annual Easter meal. Thus the events of the gospel story appear simultaneously as facts of the distant past and as phenomena that are repeated every year. In short, narrative, especially poetic, time can be unilinear as well as multilinear, it can be direct and reversed, it can be continuous and discontinuous, it can even be a combination of rectilinearity and circularity, as in the last example. I believe that it would be difficult to find another domain, except perhaps for music, where time is experienced with comparable acuity.

I am convinced that verse is maximally effective at making us experience verbal time, and this holds just as true for oral, folkloric verse as it does for written, literary verse. Verse, whether rigorously metrical or free, simultaneously carries within it both linguistic varieties of time: the time of the announcement and the announced time. Verse pertains to our immediate experience of speech activity, both motor and auditory. At the same time, we experience the structure of the verse in close connection with the semantics of the poetic text— regardless of whether there is harmony or conflict between the structure of the verse and the semantics of the text—and in this way the verse becomes an integral part

of the developing plot. It is difficult even to imagine a
sensation of the flow of time that would be more simple
and at the same time more complex, more concrete and
yet more abstract.

KP   The feelings of the great poets of the beginning of our
century towards the time factor are very characteristic.
Blok and Majakovskij, otherwise so different, both considered the element of time as the determining principle
in the creative act of making poetry. For them, rhythm
was primordial and the word secondary. In Majakovskij's
well-known pamphlet, *Kak delat' stixi* (*How to Make
Verse*), the author described his manner of beginning to
compose any poem:

> I walk along gesticulating and muttering—there are al-
> most no words yet—I slow my pace in order not to impede
> this muttering, or else I mutter more quickly, in the
> rhythm of my steps. In this way the rhythm is planed
> down and takes shape. It is the basis of any poetry and
> passes through it like a din. Gradually one is able to make
> out single words of this din. Where this fundamental
> rhythm-din comes from remains unknown. For me it is
> any repetition within myself of a sound, a noise, a rock-
> ing . . . or even the repetition of a phenomenon that I
> mark with sounds.

In his article "Poèzija zagovorov i zaklinanij" ("The
poetry of charms and incantations"), Blok speaks in his
turn of the way in which the creative force of rhythm
"carries the word on the crest of a musical wave," and
how "the rhythmic word is sharpened like an arrow that
flies directly toward its goal."

RJ   As the etymology of the Latin term *versus* itself suggests,
verse contains the idea of a regular recurrence, in contradistinction to prose, which is represented through its

etymological composition (Latin *prosa*—*provorsa*) as a movement directed forward. Verse involves the immediate sensation of the present, as well as the return of the gaze to the impulse of the preceding verses and the lively anticipation of the verses to follow. These three conjoined impressions form the active play of the invariant and the variations. They suggest to the author, to the reader, to the person reciting the lines, and to the listener the constancy of the verse measure, elaborated upon and enhanced by displacements and deviations.

The child's experience of time takes form in close contact with the development of language. Students of language acquisition by children have only recently noticed that the child often remembers an earlier stage in his progressive mastery of language. The child likes to talk about language. Metalinguistic operations are an essential instrument in his linguistic development. He recalls the past in this way: "When I was small, I talked like that, and now I speak differently, like this." He also sometimes begins to speak in the manner of a baby, either as a game or in order to solicit more tenderness or affection from adults. The phenomena that the Danish linguist Otto Jespersen (1860–1943), in his penetrating analyses of language, called "shifters" play a tremendous role in the acquisition of language by the child.

The concept of the shifter has seemed to me for some time to be one of the cornerstones of linguistics, although it has not been sufficiently appreciated in the past and therefore demands more attentive elaboration. The general meaning of the grammatical form called "shifter" is characterized by a reference back to the given speech act, the speech act that uses this form. Thus the past tense is a shifter because it literally designates an event that precedes the given act of speech. The first-person form of a verb, or the first-person pronoun, is a shifter because the basic meaning of the first person involves a reference back to the author of the given act of speech. Similarly, the second-person pronoun contains a reference to the addressee to whom the speech act in question is directed. If the addressers and addressees change in the course of the conversation, then the material content of the form *I* and *you* also changes. They shift. The desirability of including grammatical tense in linguistic usage occurs in a fairly early stage in the child's acquisition of language, at the moment when the beginner ceases to be satisfied with a direct verbal reaction to what happens before him at a given moment.

At this point, the sentence with subject and predicate first arises in his language. This allows him to attribute different predicates to a subject and to apply any predicate to different subjects. This innovation frees the child, liberating him from the *hic et nunc*, the immediate temporal and spatial circumstances. From this moment on, he can speak of events that take place at a distance from him in time and space. Along with shifts of temporal and spatial points of reference, he acquires the idea of the shifting roles of the participants in the speech events. The notion of time appears in the language of the child, as does that of spatial proximity or distance: *I* and *you*, *here* and *there*, *mine* and *yours*, *now* and *then*.

KP   It follows from what you have said that any verbal act, any phenomenon of language from phonemes to literary works, necessarily enters into a dual temporal frame: linear succession and strict simultaneity. It is here that the force as well as the relative limits of language as a means of expression reside, as noted in the dispute mentioned between Lessing and Herder.

It seems to me that the effort either to overcome these restrictions or, conversely, to utilize this frame for novel effects, determines to an important extent the development of any new form of art. The cinema, one of the most contemporary forms of art, tries most graphically to combine the simultaneous and the linear, and this is all the more striking since the cinema combines both the word and the visual image. A daring attempt in this direction is Alain Resnais's film *Last Year at Marienbad*, in which the frames of the past action "straddle" those of the present in the purely technical and cinematographic sense of the term. In this way a unity of the two components of the sign, its signifying (*signans*) and its signified (*signatum*) aspects, is created. The story is constructed around the constant interweaving of the past and the present as perceived by the heroes. One can find an analogous phenomenon among certain sculptors of today who attempt to overcome the statics of matter itself by using sculptural means to construct a set of narrative symbols that render the flow of time.

8 *THE FACTOR OF SPACE*

KP   This last set of problems, shifters and their role in the acquisition of language by the child, in fact transports us into the domain of space. You raised the question of space in relation to changes in language for the first time and in a new way in your study *K xarakteristike evrazijskogo jazykovogo sojuza* (*On the Nature of the Eurasian Linguistic Alliance*). In it you discussed the problem of the phonic evolution of language in a new light: it turns out that, in addition to the genetic factor of a common origin, linguistic change is also influenced by geographical contiguity. Neighborhood can be traded for kinship. How did you come to this idea? Did the science of the time afford theoretical bases that might have accounted for it?

RJ   There is an inevitable distance between two interlocutors, which varies depending on the person addressed by the discourse. Our linguistic means must change according to whether our dialogue is limited to our family, our neighbors, or people who come from another part of town or another region of the country. Of course, social and cultural distances must be taken into account in addition to purely spatial differences. In other words, what we encounter here is a complex of questions of geographic and social dialectology. Each of us possesses interdialectal aptitude to a greater or lesser degree. We become conscious of differences in speech between us and our interlocutors in order to understand them, and in this manner we may be said to have at least a passive mastery of certain dialects. In addition, we have a natural tendency to come somewhat closer to the manner of speaking of our interlocutor, and in this way we acquire some of the peculiarities of his dialect. Verbal exchange, which Saussurian linguistics calls speech (*parole*), is impossible without that verbal code of ours, called *langue*. Yet this code contains a number of subcodes made up of varied elements that, depending on the constantly changing context and conversational partners, we use both as addressees and addressers. Herein resides one of the conditions of the compositional multiplicity of our code, *langue*, and the speaking subject possesses the competence (precisely, *competence*) to pass freely, according to the need of the moment, from one subcode to another.

If one stops giving credence to the myth of an immobile system and includes time as an internal factor in the analysis of linguistic systems, then one should include space as well in the set of internal linguistic factors. Again we discover in the system of language a multitude of contextual variants in addition to invariants. Contextual variety refers here first of all to the diversity of the interlocutors. Beyond this, we also use dialectal variations as stylistic devices. Thus, depending on the theme and our attitudes toward it, we either fill our speech with dialectisms or carefully refrain from doing so. Only a narrow dogmatism can artificially separate the stylistic canons from the linguistic code: in reality, these canons are an integral part of the code.

Our notion of diffusion changes radically in light of these considerations. The traditional attempt to trace in principle an absolute line between two notions, the origin of a change and its expansion, no longer has any validity. Modification itself is undoubtedly and inevitably linked to expansion. If an original slip of the tongue comes to be repeated consistently in the use of its initiator and then is taken up by his environment, then and only then is it transformed from a single loose expression into the social fact of change—at first an optional change, and then, perhaps, after many years, a compulsory one.

KP   Is it possible for a single lapse to be the kernel of a modification? Consequently, is the notion well-grounded, or are there other forces that come into play here?

RJ   By "speech error" I mean a single divergence from the existing norm on the part of a speaker, but I do not raise the issue of whether this divergence has occurred purely by chance or whether there might be some element of intention in it, even unconsciously. If it is only a fortuitous and inadvertent event, then there is no reason for the speaker to repeat it or for it to be taken up by his entourage. If repetition of the error occurs and multiplies, then there can be no doubt that we are faced with a demand, although perhaps an unconscious one, for its use, although the limits assigned to this repetitive use can vary at first both in the circle of speakers and in the context of linguistic style in which the innovation takes place. The subsequent spread of the change from one style to others, and the increasing generalization of its use in the language, again presupposes the existence of a need for this innovation in the system of the language and in its speakers. One of the means facilitating the establishment, stabilization, and subsequent diffusion of an innovation is the elliptical style of speech where some element, for example a phonemic opposition, can be omitted. Moreover, such an omission, which is optional at first, can eventually become a generalized loss of a phonemic distinction in the language. Again, however, this can happen only if there is a demand for the suppression of this distinction, or dephonologization, in the system, or if there is a need to replace this phonological distinction by another that was previously redundant. This is one of the many facets of the phenomenon of transphonologization, a term I used when I treated this problem for the first time in that part of my 1923 book on Czech verse that was devoted to general phonology.

We can find particularly convincing examples of sound changes in the languages that are accessible to the continuous observation of linguists. An example is the tendency in modern French to lose the distinctive difference between tense and lax vowels, as in the pairs *saute/sotte*, *pâte/patte*. In certain dialects, this loss remains within the confines of a negligent, rapid, elliptical style of speaking, while in others it extends to all styles of speech, at least for certain pairs of words. Another characteristic example, which was already noted by French scholars at the end of the last century, is the effacement of the distinction between rounded and unrounded nasal vowels, such as *brun/brin*, *bon/ban*. A complete fulfillment of this tendency would have reduced the inventory of nasal vowels to a distinction between front and back articulation. However, only the delabialization of front vowels took place to any significant extent, a fact that can easily be explained by the secondary character of the combination of labialization and palatalization and also by the paucity of homophonous pairs that are the result of this delabialization. The loss of the rounded-unrounded distinction among nasal back vowels did not experience a parallel extension and has survived only in the narrow confines of a negligent manner of speaking. There are two reasons for this: the primary (unmarked) character of the combination of rounding and backness in vowels, and the abundance of homophones arising from this change (for example, *cheveux blonds* becomes homophonous with *cheveux blancs*, which may lead to misunderstandings).

Upon tracing the history of the phonic and grammatical modifications of different languages, I became increasingly convinced of the necessity of constantly combining two opposite forces: the tendency to maintain an equilibrium and the tendency to destroy it. This is the essence of the self-motion of language. The principal vehicle for the displacements of the equilibrium are the elliptical and expressive aspects of language. The changes that attempt to reestablish the destroyed equilibrium in the system of language play an essential role in the passage from the old order to the new. In this respect, the habitual comparisons between the evolution of language and a game of chess are very convincing.

Of course, a speech lapse can be initiated by different individuals and even in a number of different places, but once again one is faced with internal linguistic preconditions that encourage the multiple occurrence and multiple incorporation of the innovation.

In the same way, there can be competition between acceptance and rejection of an innovation in both its place of origin and a secondary larger area. Each linguistic community, and each member of the community, possesses a certain degree of conformity: the basic question concerns the choice between a temporal and spatial type of conformism. In order to draw closer to its neighbors, a community assimilates an element of language that has already taken root in surrounding communities, that is, an element that will facilitate mutual communication and bring the two groups closer together. The spatial conformists who adopt this sort of innovation deny the tradition of their own language and are consequently nonconformist in the temporal order. The opposite phenomenon, the refusal to assimilate a neighboring linguistic acquisition in the name of safeguarding one's own tradition, provides an example of the reverse: temporal conformism and spatial nonconformism.

The spatial conformism in question is not limited to interdialectal relations, but extends to relations between neighboring languages as well. In the present century, the science of language has seriously faced for the first time the problem that the features characteristic of a linguistic family can extend beyond the limits of that family. Such an extension often turns out to affect languages that are distant in structure and origin, although sometimes these effects are limited to only one part of a given geographic area. The observation of this phenomenon led to the acceptance of the term "language alliance," coined and proposed by Trubetzkoy at the International Congress of Linguists at The Hague in 1928, and to the development of this concept in relation to morphology and syntax as well as to phonic structure. It is curious that interlingual structural particularities soon attracted the attention of American inquirers into the indigenous languages of America and Africa, while remaining mostly unnoticed in the languages of the Eurasian continent.

Even so eminent an observer as Franz Boas (1858–1942), who revealed the existence of phonic and grammatical phenomena common to the Amerindian languages and encompassing large zones of these languages without regard to origin, understood that these common traits were not indications of a genetic community, although he believed that such an interlingual expansion was specific to the American and African languages alone. You can imagine his suprise and joy when I presented him with work on phonological language alliances that I had observed in the Old World.

In the thirties I published a number of studies proving the existence of a vast "Eurasian linguistic alliance," which encompassed Russian, the other languages of Eastern Europe, and the majority of the Uralic and Altaic languages, all of which make use of the phonemic opposition of palatalized and nonpalatalized consonants. I also characterized in passing the Circumbaltic languages, which possess a phonemic opposition of two types of word intonation.

At first, my publications and presentations on this topic provoked virulent criticism from the philological authorities. They accepted the evidence I had assembled, but refused to attribute any scientific significance to these indications of community; they judged that these examples, although numerous, were merely fortuitous. In a published discussion, the eminent Dutch linguist Nicolaas van Wijk (1880–1941) accepted the data that I had observed, but accompanied his acceptance with an embarrassing question: how were these phenomena to be explained? Today the idea of language alliance, on the grammatical as well as the phonological level, has gained wide acceptance. But this does not preclude the continued existence of silent opposition to the suggestion that the traditional, purely genetic, view of linguistic filiation must be supplemented by a geographically-based conception of acquired (rather than inherent) affinity. Since that time, science has accomplished a good deal in discovering and exactly specifying different phonological and grammatical alliances, but there unfortunately remain deplorable obstacles, such as the lack of phonological atlases, which continue to slow the development of this research.

It should no longer seem enigmatic that such alliances appear so frequently and still exist. We have already mentioned common examples of a complete or partial fusion of different dialects in individual usage. To this, one should add the well-known yet insufficiently studied phenomena of bilingualism, the mutual and internalized equivalence of value between two languages within the linguistic thought of a single individual. One can observe a rather wide diversity in the alternating usage of the two languages, in their fusion and relative delimitation.

In the Russian intelligentsia of my generation, for example, people pass easily from Russian to French and back in conversation among coevals. They sometimes include French phrases in their Russian utterances, and sometimes insert Russian words and expressions when speaking French. Gallicisms were perfectly natural in the colloquial language of Russians from the period described by Tolstoj in *War and Peace* until the recent past. For the characters in that historical novel, French was not a foreign language. It was just one style among many of Russian speech. On the other hand, those same Russians who also spoke German would not usually admit, from the point of view of style, the direct insertion of Germanisms into a Russian sentence. The border between those two languages was clearly drawn. Gallicisms, however, were not limited to the lexicon and phraseology of the language of the Russian nobility, but often directly affected the sounds of speech: for example, in *Eugene Onegin* Pushkin notes the ability of upper-class people to change the Russian phoneme sequence of vowel + nasal consonant into a French nasalized vowel.

People who speak the language of a neighboring country and who can communicate intimately with its inhabitants and translate from that language to their own and back are often held in high regard by their compatriots. As if to show off their thorough knowledge of the language of their neighbors, these speakers often transfer to their own tongue phonic or grammatical features of the foreign language. These borrowings, which at first are stylistic in nature, become emblems, as it were, of the broadened linguistic horizon of these bilinguals and are easily imitated by the unilingual compatriots. Although this imitation affects at the outset only some isolated elements, bit by bit it is transformed into a fashion, which eventually acquires full citizenship and becomes an integral part of the mother tongue. Thus is a language alliance engendered.

The principles underlying the choice of features that constitute this alliance are interesting. Why did a genetically dissimilar evolution, but a common structure of prosodic elements, lie at the base of the alliance of the languages around the Baltic? Why was the distinctive function of consonant palatalization chosen to constitute the alliance of the languages that are labeled Eurasian? This selection of features, and the direction and limits of expansion, are all problems that require new approaches and criteria in linguistics, as well as interdisciplinary interpretation. With every step, one finds in the ever-growing number of these secondary linguistic affinities (*Wahlverwandschaften*) an entire series of problems which have yet to be resolved. In much that at one time appeared to be a mosaic of chance events we now perceive geo-linguistic regularities awaiting explanation.

Only the creation of atlases will oblige linguists to reflect in a consistent manner upon such isoglosses as the boundary line that runs between the Western European mass of languages with articles and the Eastern European languages without articles. What is especially interesting is that the Scandinavian languages to the north and the Balkan languages (Rumanian, Bulgarian) to the south are border languages, in that they display a postpositional article, in contradistinction to all the other languages of Western Europe that have a prepositional article. What is the origin of this shared feature in two groups of languages, one of which is due north and the other due south of the boundary between the languages that have and do not have articles? I would like to repeat here the words of Joseph de Maistre (1753–1821) which I quoted at the end of my volume *Word and Language* (*Selected Writings* II): "Let us never speak of *chance.* . . ." It is not difficult to explain the in-between position occupied by languages with postpositional articles: the prepositional article functions as an independent word (compare *the boy* and *the young boy*), whereas the postpositional article is a simple suffix. Thus what languages with postpositional articles have in common with languages without articles is the absence of a freely *separable* word-article.

One should point out that it is impossible to establish any connection between the diffusion of phonic and grammatical features and the sociocultural dominance of the language that serves as the source or model for these features. It would be erroneous to suppose that the languages of culturally, sociopolitically, or economically dominant countries necessarily prevail over the language of countries that are weaker and more dependent in any of these respects. Quite often, linguistic influence passes from the weaker side to the stronger. We should also point out that these widespread isoglosses generally coincide with other similarly puzzling lines encountered in the geographical distribution of anthropological traits. These often unexpected connections require a many-sided analysis in accordance with the methodogical theses advanced by the ingenious scholar Petr Nikolaevich Savickij, the precursor of structural geography.

If alliances between languages are the extreme manifestation of linguistic conformism, one can also see in interlingual relations the opposite phenomenon, nonconformism. Languages that run the risk of being submerged in neighboring languages sometimes develop specific features to distinguish themselves sharply from the structure of their threatening neighbors. It is for this reason that Lusatian-Sorbian and Slovenian—the only Slavic languages that ran the risk of being Germanicized or Italianized—have conserved and even partially developed in their morphological system the category of the dual number. All past and present attempts to exclude questions of time and space from the study of the linguistic system impoverish and destroy the vital principle of the linguistic system itself, which inevitably includes the vast subject matter of time and space.

KP   Among Russian scholars in the West, one could observe
at that time a heightened interest in the diverse functions
of geographic space. The volume *Tridcatye Gody* (*The
Thirties*), published in 1931 by the Russian Eurasians, a
cultural trend developed in the 1920s in Sofia by Russian
émigré scholars who proposed that Russia should be considered as an distinct continent of the world—Eurasia—
different in many respects from both Europe and Asia,
contains a study by Ivan Savel'ev, actually Petr Grigor'
evich Bogatyrev , on the role of isoglosses in folklore.
The ideas that he presents on the diffusion and hybrid-
ization of the Russian oral tradition coincide methodologically with the problems of language alliances.
Published in the same collection was a chapter of P. N.
Savickij's book on structural geography, in which he considers the peculiarities and function of the vast "continuous space" occupied by Russia and now by the Soviet
Union. The ethnographer E. D. Khara-Davan analyzed
the functions of the space of the steppe in the customs
and development of physical features of the nomadic
peoples of that area. In spite of its pioneering role in the
further development of the linguistic ideas of affinity,
intercommunication, and evolution of languages, your *K
xarakteristike evrazijskogo jazykovogo sojuza* (*Towards a
Characterization of the Eurasian Language Alliance*) is
much indebted to this set of ideas and in turn exercised
a noticeable influence on their development.

9 *TIME IN THE FRAMEWORK OF SIGNS*

KP   Your remarks on the role of time and space in phono-
      logical and grammatical analysis lead us to the even more
      complex problem of the relation between time and verbal
      signs, and from there to the theme of time in its relation
      to signs in general.

RJ   Charles Sanders Peirce (1839–1914), the greatest Amer-
      ican philosopher, addressed what is perhaps the most
      essential and fruitful question of language and time in
      his framework of three types of signs. On the one hand,
      Peirce singled out the "index" and the "icon," both of
      which are based on an actual link between *signans* and
      signatum. An index connects the *signans* to the *signatum*
      by virtue of the actual contiguity between the two, while
      an icon connects the two entities by virtue of their actual
      similarity. In contradistinction to these two types of signs,
      Peirce delimits a third: the "symbol," which is based not
      on an actual relation between *signans* and *signatum*, but
      on a prescribed, conventional, and learned relation be-
      tween them. In Peirce's terminology, the symbol relates
      the *signans* to the *signatum* by virtue of a prescribed and
      conventional contiguity between these two entities. Ac-
      cording to Peirce's theory, the symbol, as opposed to either
      the index or the icon, is not an object but only a "frame
      law," which gives rise to different contextual applications
      in what Peirce calls "occurrences." In the system of con-
      cepts and terms established by Peirce, the signs of lan-
      guage are essentially symbols that also contain some
      iconic and indexical elements.
         Peirce's reflections on the three categories of signs and
      their relation to the problem of time are particularly wor-
      thy of note. In his study entitled *My Masterpiece*, he con-
      ceives the icon as being the accomplished image of an

experience that is already past, while the index is linked to an ongoing experience in the present. The symbol, however, always possesses a general meaning and is based on a general law; everything that is truly general is related to the indefinite future. The past is an accomplished fact, whereas a general law cannot ever be totally accomplished. It is a potentiality whose mode is the *esse in futuro*.

The value of a symbol, and a linguistic symbol in particular, lies in the fact that it "gives us the possibility of predicting the future." The word and the future are indissolubly linked—that is one of Peirce's most penetrating theses. For it is clear that the frame law is only a condition for all possible future occurrences, and that it is in the context of each occurrence that the verbal invariant of the verbal sign—its general meaning—acquires its new, particular meaning. The context is variable, and the particular meaning of the word undergoes renewal in each new context: herein lies the creative power of the verbal sign. Through this creative force, the sign opens a path toward the indefinite future, that is, it anticipates, it predicts things to come. These brief theses encapsulate the essence of the science of creative language in general, and of poetic language in particular.

10 *THE CONCEPT OF THE MARK*

KP   Speaking of Peirce and the application of his classification of signs to language leads us back to the question of markedness in language. It follows from Peirce's system that the symbolic function figures as an unmarked category in relation to the index on the one hand and the icon on the other. This question is indissolubly linked to the problem of binarism, which we discussed above. If one considers the development of your system today, the question of hierarchy seems inseparable from that of binarism, yet the idea of markedness did not arise until a little later than the question of binarism. It was only in a letter written in 1930 that Trubetzkoy first started a discussion of markedness in phonology.

    It would be interesting to know how this concept arose and developed. It is now also being increasingly applied in domains of language other than phonology and grammar, a phenomenon which you yourself noticed at the time, especially in relation to social anthropology and psychology. Already in your answer to that letter of Trubetzkoy's you made the instructive remark that "for Majakovskij, life was a marked category that could only be realized when there was a motivation for it; for him it was life, rather than death, which required motivation." The application of the notion of markedness to literary prose seems to be most promising.

RJ   From the beginning, the hierarchy of values and the hierarchical relation between two terms of an opposition were important in my scientific reflections and writings. The multivalued hierarchical order appeared in the forefront in verse and its interpretation, and revealed ever more clearly a gradation of two-valued relations. From the beginning of the twenties on, I used the term and the concept of "marked time," which had played such a pertinent role in P. Verrier's *Essay on the Principles of English Metrics*, a work that I had studied. This constituent of subjective time, which is correlative to unmarked time and which in verse is superimposed on the time of the objective duration of the recited poem, provided me with the key to understanding the reciprocal relation between meter and rhythm, which at the time was the subject of much controversy. The opposition of the marked and the unmarked furnished me with the means of developing the urgent problem of variants and invariants in the study of verse.

In my first book, *Novejšaja russkaja poèzija* (*Recent Russian Poetry*), written in Moscow in the spring of 1919 and published in Prague on the threshold of 1921, I touched upon the same topic of the fundamental difference between two, it would seem, empirically equivalent concepts: the natural, unmarked nakedness of the cave dweller and the disrobing of a European of the Victorian era. The juxtaposition of marked and unmarked components allowed me to develop the urgent problem of invariants and variation in the study of verse. The concept of paired hierarchical relations was in the air, but still required logical explanation and technical inferences.

In July 1930, as he was preparing a lecture on phonemic systems for the international phonological conference that the Prague Circle convoked for that December, Trubetzkoy wrote to me that he had found an "important gap" that both of us had tolerated in our theory of correlative phonemes: "It concerns the *conceptual content*, so to speak, of the correlation." Trubetzkoy realized that the binary opposition assumes a particular form in linguistic consciousness: "The presence of some mark is opposed to its absence (or the maximum of some mark to its minimum)." He came to the conclusion that "only one of the terms of a correlation is perceived as actively modified and as positively possessing some mark, while the other term is perceived as passively unmodified and as lacking the mark." The problem of marked and unmarked elements was raised at the Prague conference both in Trubetzkoy's lecture on phonological systems and in mine on prosodic structures. In November I made the following response to Trubetzkoy's letter:

I am increasingly convinced that your notion of correlation always being a relation of a marked and an unmarked series is one of your most remarkable and productive ideas. I think that it will become important not only for linguistics, but also for ethnology and the history of culture, and that correlations encountered in the history of culture, such as life/death, liberty/oppression, sin/virtue, holidays/workdays, etc., can always be reduced to the relation a/not a; the relevant thing is to establish what constitutes the marked set for each period, group, people, and so on. I am convinced that many ethnographic phenomena which seem at first glance to be identical, such as conceptions of the world, are actually distinguished by the fact that what is considered marked in one system is considered unmarked in the other.

At that time we were both deeply affected by Majakovskij's suicide, which took place in April of 1930. We understood his lines about unmarked, "easy" death, and about the fact that "to make a life is markedly more difficult," and we realized that, according to this upside-down view of the world, not death but life "required motivation." In a series of subsequent studies continuing to the present, I have examined the relationship between the marked and the unmarked in the opposition of distinctive features, and I have attempted to establish the dependence of these relations on the structure of the whole phonological system. It became ever clearer through this study that the place of the marked and unmarked term depended first on the composition of the entire bundle of distinctive features. For instance, in the fundamental opposition between the compact and the diffuse, the first is marked in consonants and the second in vowels—a difference easily explained by the fact that optimal vowels are compact and optimal consonants diffuse. The famous thesis of Antoine Meillet (1866–1936), which I used as the epigraph to my *Remarks on Phonological Evolution*, finds full application here: "Every linguistic fact is part of a whole in which all parts are interrelated" ("Chaque fait linguistique fait parti d'un ensemble où tout se tient"). It has been only in the last ten years that the "intrinsic content" of phonological oppositions, that is to say, the place and character of their specific marks, has been a topic of interest in America.

In an article in 1931 on the structure of the Russian verb I began to transfer the same opposition of marked and unmarked into the domain of grammar, and in particular into morphological structure, and I have continued in this direction to the present. It has become quite clear to me that the most complicated systems of declension and conjugation, to mention only those two paradigms, display a clear and simple logic when they are properly decomposed into a hierarchical ensemble of pairs of marked and unmarked components in opposition to each other. This method is particularly fruitful for the comparative study of different grammatical systems, which in turn facilitates its application to the grammar of individual languages. The morphological typology of languages, that old dream of linguists, has now acquired solid foundations and appears as well to enable us to explain and define more rigorously the universals of grammar.

The conception of binary opposition at any level of the linguistic system as a relation between a mark and the absence of this mark carries to its logical conclusion the idea that a hierarchical order underlies the entire linguistic system in all its ramifications. In spite of the doubts of skeptics, the distribution of the marked and unmarked series in binary oppositions cannot be regarded as a subjective operation on the part of the intepreters but is instead given directly in the linguistic system itself, and the process whereby it is abstracted on the basis of linguistic analysis is a fully objective procedure. There of course exist pairs of members of an opposition that present difficulties to the analyst with regard to the place of the mark in a given binary opposition, but, as shown in a number of examples, this difficulty is being overcome as the analysis becomes more accurate.

On the phonological level, the position of the marked term in any given opposition is determined by the relation of this opposition to the other oppositions in the phonological system—in other words, to the distinctive features that are either simultaneously or temporally contiguous. In grammatical oppositions, however, the distinction between marked and unmarked terms lies in the area of the general meaning of each of the juxtaposed forms. The general meaning of the marked term is characterized by the conveyance of more precise, specific, and additional information than the unmarked term. For example, in languages containing an opposition between the two grammatical tenses of past and present, the former is always marked and the latter unmarked. The general meaning of the past lies in the fact that the announced act precedes the act of announcement in time, while the general meaning of the present does not establish a temporal relation between the two acts. The latter grammatical category can, therefore, be used in language to designate any of the following: an announced act taking place at the same time as the announcement, constant action unlimited in time, an act preceding the announcement ("In 1821 Napoleon dies"), or, finally, an event in the future ("I am leaving town tomorrow"). On the other hand, except for a few extremely figurative usages, the past can only be utilized to designate actions in the past, as Lucien Tesnière (1893–1954), a champion of structural linguistics who was closely linked to the program of the Prague Linguistic Circle, tried to demonstrate. He almost managed to construct on this basis a system for the French verb and even a set of principles of general syntax. Today these problems are receiving much attention, which will no doubt advance the development of the primary objectives of the analysis and provide explanations for the essence of grammatical structure. However, this will happen only on condition that the connection between differentiated grammatical processes and correspondingly different grammatical concepts is taken into account, for this connection is important both for language itself and for its investigation.

11 PARALLELISM

KP   The question of binarism and of the marked elements of
the system leads us to the theme of parallelism—a capital,
probably even primordial, element of literary art. It was
also one of your first scientific passions. Parallelism is a
binary combination. You have always specified that parallelism is an equivalence, not an identity, but the concept
of equivalence in turn seems to blur the inequality of
the two terms and to level the hierarchical primacy of
one of them. How is one to treat the marked term of the
pair in this case?

    And one other important question: how is the choice
of the equivalent elements to be made? In your fundamental study, "Grammatical Parallelism and Its Russian
Facet," published in *Language* in 1966, you approach the
problem indirectly through questions that are at the same
time directives: "[One must establish] whether, to what
extent, and in what regard the entities that correspond
in their positions are mutually similar," and, "What
are . . . the categories that can become equivalent within
the schema in question."

    You clearly showed that "certain types of similarity
are obligatory, or else quite preferable," in the example
of a variant of a seventeenth-century narrative, *Gore-
zločast'e (Sorrow-Misfortune)*, which you studied for years.
Yet there seem to be a number of cases in which the
examiner has difficulty in defining the semantic basis of
the constant elements of a couple, or even in discovering
where the parallelism lies. This is clearly evident in the
recent and splendid work of James Fox, *The Comparative
Study of Parallelisms*, in which he attempts to decipher
the extremely complex semantics of the continuous parallelisms of the folk poetry of Rotinese. The study of

these questions has taken a captivating turn, and promises a series of new discoveries and also, perhaps, new methodological directives. On the other hand, parallelism itself is difficult to determine in newer, particularly poetic, texts. In contradistinction to folklore, these texts have no continuous system of couples, and the inquirer is sometimes condemned to intuitive surmises in determining paired equivalents.

Through what stages did your investigation of parallelism pass? How did questions of phonology influence this study? You once mentioned that you had already begun to analyze the song *Gore* in Baku in 1917.

RJ   Apparently there has been no other subject during my entire scholarly life that has captured me as persistently as have the questions of parallelism. At the meetings of the newborn Moscow Linguistic Circle in the spring of 1915, we analyzed and discussed the verse of Russian folklore in its recitative variety, especially the epic, which seemed the most original, and, as we already suspected, the most archaic, form in all of Russian folk poetry. We studied the epic texts written down in the remarkable eighteenth-century collection attributed to Kirsha Danilov (whose name figures in the manuscript). Also in 1915, Moscow University proposed as the topic of research for the prize named for the celebrated linguist and folklorist Fedor Ivanovich Buslaev the language of the epic poems of northern Russia called *byliny*. These epics had been recorded at the beginning of this century in the basin of the Mezen River by Alexandr Dmitrievich Grigor'ev (1874–1945). As I worked on these texts, I once again encountered the various problems of Russian oral epic verse that had been raised by Fedor Evgen'evich Korsh

(1843–1915) in his penetrating sketches, but which none-theless were far from being definitely solved. Finally, still in 1915, I had the opportunity of hearing Marija Krivopolenova (1843–1924), the magnificent old folksinger and storyteller who had been brought to Moscow from the Arkhangelsk province. Hearing and studying her recitation provided me with the chance to verify my observations on epic verse with the actual performance of an outstanding carrier of the oral tradition.

I was to return a number of times to questions of Russian *byliny*. The step-by-step application of comparative analysis enabled me to derive the prosodic structure of the *byliny* first from that of Common Slavic verse, and subsequently from Indo-European versification. On the other hand, my research on the plots of the *byliny* helped me to determine their ancient roots and especially their historical and mythological substratum. But my study of the Russian oral tradition was not limited to these questions alone.

From my student years, I have been struck by the internal structure evident in the recitative verse of the Russian oral epic tradition, namely by that parallelism which ties together contiguous verses from beginning to end. I was particularly astonished to realize that this important point seemed hardly to interest the specialists in Russian folklore. The organization of texts into couplets was well known from Biblical versification—the very term "parallelism" had been introduced to describe it two hundred years earlier—and the equally consistent parallelism of Finnish epic verse was often compared to it. Although the parallelism of Russian poetry closely follows these systems, it is freer and more varied. In 1917

I undertook to analyze along these lines a single text which was included in Kirsha Danilov's collection and which stands on the boundary between lyrical and epic poetry. It was a short specimen (twenty-one lines) of the remarkable cycle of poems on misfortune. I promised to contribute an article on the subject to the forthcoming issue of the *Sbornik po teorii poètičeskogo jazyka* (*Collection on the Theory of Poetic Language*), which the OPOJAZ was preparing at the time. The issue appeared in 1919, but without my article, which I rightly considered as an immature sketch that needed extension and revision in light of more precise principles of linguistic analysis. I allowed this analysis of these twenty-one lines of the "Misfortune" poem to ripen for half a century before using it in my monograph on grammmatical parallelism and its Russian facet, published in 1966 in the American periodical *Language*. Even this monograph is in my eyes only a preliminary sketch.

In 1865, a hundred years before my own endeavors, one of the most fascinating poets of the last century, Gerard Manley Hopkins (1844–1889), wrote while still a young student that "the artificial part of poetry, perhaps we shall be right to say all artifice, reduces itself to the principle of parallelism. The structure of poetry is that of continuous parallelism, ranging from the technical so-called parallelism of Hebrew poetry and the antiphones of Church music up to the intricacy of Greek or Italian or English verse." Hopkins was right in believing that the important part played by the parallelism of expression in our poetry "will surprise anyone when first pointed out."

There is a system of steady correspondences in composition and order of elements on many different levels:

syntactic constructions, grammatical forms and grammatical categories, lexical synonyms and total lexical
identities, and finally combinations of sounds and prosodic schemes. This system confers upon the lines connected through parallelism both clear uniformity and
great diversity. Against the background of the integral
matrix, the effect of the variations of phonic, grammatical,
and lexical forms and meanings appears particularly
eloquent.

In my review of the study by Wolfgang Steinitz
(1905–1967) of parallelism in Finno-Karelian folk poetry
(Helsinki, 1936), which opened new vistas on the subject,
I noted that the analysis needed further development. In
particular, pairs of seemingly unrelated lines frequently
reveal special parallelistic connections that the inquirer
has not yet noticed. Against the background of constant
variation, the repeated units become incomparably more
striking. By focusing on parallelisms and similarities in
pairs of lines, one is led to pay more attention to every
similarity and every difference that occurs between contiguous couplets of verse and between hemistichs within
a single line. In other words, this approach confers particular importance on each similarity and on each contrast. One experiences the link between the external form
and the signification. The perception of similarities and
contiguities within the couplet united by parallelism leads
automatically to the need to find an answer to the unconscious questions: what links the two lines? Is it an
association by similarity or by contrast? Or is it an association through contiguity, and, if so, is it a contiguity
in time or in space? All of which leads finally to the
essential question for the comprehension of the verse:

what is the hierarchical relation between the parallel units? Which of them is subordinated to the other? How is the relation in question actualized—by the internal content of the verse, or by the fact that one of the lines simply dominates the other, or finally by the position that the couplet occupies in the whole?

This rich orchestration of parts and of the whole should put to rest once and for all the empty remarks about the poverty and monotony of systems of parallelism in verse. The great possibilities inherent in close poetic combination of similarities and contrasts account for the widespread diffusion, and perhaps the predominant role, of systems of parallelism in all poetry, both oral and written. (One has but to recall the numerous centuries of the predominance of parallelism in Chinese versification.) Throughout the world, inquirers are constantly finding new systems of verbal art based on canonic parallelism. Moreover, through anthropological research assimilating the principles of linguistic methodology, such as that of James Fox, we are discovering the existence of close ties between parallelism in poetry and in mythology, including ritual. The role played by parallelism in the tradition and creation of myth reveals ever new and unexpected possibilities in the structural properties of parallelism. This role brings out in particular the significance of binary structures at different levels of cultural anthropology, thus still opening new vistas for an interdisciplinary study of parallelism.

Let us return to that urgent task set out for us by Hopkins: to proceed to a more generalized study of parallelism, even in the systems of poetry where there is no canonic parallelism and where only a latent principle of parallel construction is at work. We should take note here of the fruitful experience of Saussure in his remarkable digressions into "phonic poetics" which he described in his monumental work on anagrams (although, unfortunately, only a few extracts from this work have been published). This voluminous manuscript clearly shows that, unlike either ordinary language or canonic parallelism, these poetic structures break with the principle of "consecutivity" in time, in order that the system of phonic and grammatical correspondences, and especially binary correspondences, can be very freely distributed. In the words of Saussure, "it must be granted from the outset that we can jump ahead from one member of the pair and find its correspondent in the next line, or even several lines later." In addition, there arises in these circumstances an opposition between paired units and those that actually lack a correspondent, i.e., units which, by virtue of their singularity, stand out strikingly against the background of paired elements that predominate in the text.

KP   What is the role of parallelism in literary prose, beyond the obvious cases of rhythmic prose or Biblical prose? Some scholars consider that your principle of all-encompassing parallelistic structures in poetry can be extended to prose, with the difference that in prose this principle applies to larger components than in poetry. Others think on the contrary that the presence of parallelism in prose contradicts your own definition of prose as a primarily metonymic construction and of poetry as a primarily metaphoric one. It is clear, of course, that parallelism does exist in prose. Even the earliest Formalists took note of this fact—some of them only clumsily so, and others, like Petr M. Bicilli (1878–1953), with much greater subtlety. The components that they distinguished as obligatorily paired were primarily characters in different works who were possessed of contrasting personality traits. In addition to these obvious components, it is easy to find other, more abstract thematic units. One can even find that the entire subject matter of a work is given a parallelistic structure, as in the parodies of Gogol or the moral tales of Tolstoj. But in one way or another these examples are connected with folklore. I would like to pose the question in a more systematic and principled fashion: can one consider that with regard to parallelism there is a certain sharp boundary between *versus* and *provorsa*, particularly in light of your theory of prose as a structure based on the principle of contiguity and poetry as a structure founded on the principle of similarity?

RJ   The role of parallelism extends far beyond the confines of poetic language. A number of types of literary prose are constructed according to a strict principle of parallelism, but here too one can apply *mutatis mutandis* the remark of Hopkins that the scholar will be amazed to discover the presence of an underlying and latent parallelism even in the relatively free composition of works of prose, where the structures in parallel assume an irregular appearance and deviate maximally from total submission to the elementary principle of succession in time. Nonetheless, there is a notable hierarchical difference between the parallelism of verse and that of prose. In poetry, it is the verse itself that dictates the structure of parallelism. The prosodic structure of the verse as a whole, the melodic unity and the repetition of the line and of its metrical constituents determine the parallel distribution of elements of grammatical and lexical semantics, and, inevitably, the sound organizes the meaning. Inversely, in prose semantic units differing in extent play the primary role in organizing parallel structures. In this case, the parallelism of units connected by similarity, contrast, or contiguity actively influences the composition of the plot, the characterization of the subjects and objects of the action, and the sequence of themes in the narrative.

Literary prose lies between poetry as such and the language of ordinary practical communication, and one should keep in mind the fact that it is infinitely more difficult to analyze an intermediate phenomenon than it is to study polar opposites. This does not mean, of course, that one should refuse to study the structural properties of narration in prose. It is rather a question of refining one's methods and keeping sight of the fact that there is no single literary prose, as such, but only a series of degrees that bring it closer to one of the extremes in question while pulling it away from the other. In particular, we should take as our immediate goal the determination of the specificity of folkloric prose, which is much more stable and transparent than individualized literary prose with its great variety of stylistic orientations. The closer individual prose comes to folklore, the more it is dominated by parallelisms. In 1862 the question was raised by Lev Tolstoj in a programmatic article: "Who should learn to write from whom: should we teach the children of peasants to write, or should peasant children teach us to write?" He insisted that the stories of children surpassed the masterpieces of Goethe, and he tried to approach the "wisdom of children" in works of his own—

works in which the immediacy of parallelistic devices stands out with the elementary precision of folklore.

Of course, phonic structures and prosodic means in particular create a favorable condition for the perceptibility of poetic parallelism, while frequently hiding the incentive itself. For example, when I first read "Misfortune" in the collection of Kirsha Danilov, I did not immediately notice the way in which parallel lines and couplets were highlighted in the text. In the first half of the poem contiguous couplets are contrasted, in the second half, contiguous verses. The first part of the poem, which is formulated with impersonal expressions, presents a regular alternation between couplets in which one of the two initial downbeats falls on the final stressed syllable of the word, and couplets without this word stress. In the second part, which is personal, the alternation is between lines in which the first downbeat falls on a final stressed syllable, and lines in which the ictus falls on a penultimate stressed syllable. Thus I was able once again to convince myself of the correctness of Lev Vladimirovich Shcherba's idea that philology is factually the science of slow and repeated reading. Clearly, this systematic and contrastive distribution of accents and word boundaries focusses attention on the varied manifestations of sound-and-sense parallelism. In turn, poetic parallelism provides valuable support for the linguistic analysis of language. It accomplishes this by indicating precisely which grammatical categories or which constituents of syntactic structures are perceived as equivalent by a given linguistic community, and, consequently, can assume the role of parallel units. For example, in both Slavic and Biblical texts the vocative and the imperative can occupy corresponding positions in parallel phrases; that is, in addition to the distinction between the form of the noun and the form of the verb, the common conative character of the two categories manifests itself as a parallel feature. In the same way, the parallelism of two sentences is unaffected even if one of the sentences contains a predicating verb and the other elliptically omits the predicate and thus gives place to a zero predicate.

Grammatical parallelism can be a precious aid to the scholar who wants to study poetic parallelism in systems of language that are far removed from his own. It allows him to determine the fundamental grammatical features which underlie the system that at first seems so convoluted. Semantic comparisons applicable in a given parallelistic system furnish a key not only for understanding the semantic turn of the language in question, but also for comprehending the particularities of the linguistic thought of the community, although great caution must certainly be observed when drawing inferences about thought from the facts of language. In any case, the different analyses of parallelism in millenia-old Chinese poetry have been richly instructive concerning conclusions and the possibility of new discoveries.

12 POETRY AND GRAMMAR

KP   You mention grammatical categories among the elements that can form couples of equivalence. Your innovative contribution to poetics, especially in the years you have spent in America, lies in the study of the particular role of grammar in poetry. It would seem you were already interested in these questions during your sojourn in Czechoslovakia, when you were editing the translation of Pushkin into Czech. It was probably at that time that the idea occurred to you that it was impossible to translate certain categories from one given language to another. Your 1959 article "On Linguistic Aspects of Translation" takes up this idea and transforms it into a specific theoretical problem. In this article, you speak of the "interpretation" of linguistic units (code-units) in translation, rather than their literal transposition. Still later, in a theoretical article that reflects the experience of analyses of texts in a great many languages, "Poetry of Grammar and Grammar of Poetry" (1968), you develop the idea held by American linguists concerning the obligatory character of grammatical categories in any given language. There seems to be a close tie between the compulsory character of these categories and the impossibility of translating them. Did this complex of ideas provide the starting point for your definitive conclusions on the special role of grammar in poetry?

RJ   In fact, a number of circumstances led me to the problem of grammar in poetry, beginning with the difficulties I encountered in editing those Czech translations of the lyrical, epic, and dramatic verse of Pushkin that were to be published on the hundredth anniversary of the poet's death in 1837. These translations, which had been prepared by the best poets of Czechoslovakia, seemed at first to have rendered precisely all the features of the originals: the meter, the system of rhymes, the tropes and figures, and the basic style. Yet there was clearly an awkwardness to the translations.

In comparing the mastery manifested in one of Pushkin's greatest poems, "The Bronze Horseman," to the Czech version by Bohumil Mathesius (1888–1952) and to the Polish version by the outstanding translator and poet Julian Tuwim (1894–1953), I felt most acutely that there was something amiss, something that tarnished the strongest lines of the original. The autonomous role of the grammatical framework in verse systems based on grammatical parallelism provided me with a convincing hint as to where to look for an answer. The manuals on the theory of literature that we read in our school years spoke of a poetry without images, in which the ideas and emotional content alone seemed to constitute the value of a text. But it is linguistics that has come to our aid here, by opening our eyes to the fundamental role that the selection and the organization of grammatical meanings play in our linguistic thought and in verbal communication.

The study of rhyme that I began in 1919 focused first on instances in Khlebnikov's verse and then later on examples of that of Majakovskij. This study, by the way, was first conducted with Majakovskij around a garden table at our common *dacha*, thus providing me with the opportunity to discuss poetic devices with the poet himself. This research demonstrated the close connection between questions of verse and its sounds on the one hand and problems of grammar on the other. It was in that same village of Pushkino, where Majakovskij would soon undertake his "dialogue with the sun," that I realized that there existed no agrammatism in rhyme, only two poles: grammatical rhyme, based on a combination of sound correspondence and morphological kinship or identity, and antigrammatical rhyme, which opposed this combination in various ways. Between the two poles, finally, existed different transitional types of rhyme. It was important to realize that the relation to grammar was experienced with no less force in antigrammatical rhyme than in grammatical rhyme, and that it was dissimilarity no less than coincidence that gave rise to the simultaneous presence of the phonic plane and the grammatical one.

At the end of the 1950s I approached some of the fundamental questions raised by the interaction of linguistics and poetics. I presented the general problems of such a study on several occasions, and finally surveyed them in the collection *Style in Language*. Subsequently I concentrated on the distribution and artistic function of the different grammatical categories within single poetic works and was surprised to observe from the outset the symmetry and regularity of grammatical oppositions among the most diverse poets, from every period and every language. At each step it became clearer that grammatical categories, whether reiterative or contrasting, had a compositional function.

Hopkins's "figures of grammar" were just as significant, vital, and effective in poetic art as were the "figures of sound." In order to avoid any partiality I would take texts at random, or I would analyze examples mentioned by my skeptical students or colleagues as inappropriate for such an analysis. At the beginning, many listeners to my lectures on this subject refused to believe that these grammatical figures could exist in the work of such diverse poets. After one of my lectures, a professor of English literature told me he was quite sure that it was impossible to detect such a poetic organization of the grammatical categories in, for example, Shakespeare's sonnet #129. That same evening I began to study those lines, and shortly thereafter, jointly with Lawrence Jones, I published the results of this research, based on the unambiguous and precise data that we naturally found in this sonnet. These results were further sharpened in a masterful paper and table by Ivor Richards (1893–1979) who was both a scholar and a poet. I had occasion to publish in the scholarly journals of many different countries my grammatical analyses of verse in English, German, French, Italian, Portuguese, Rumanian, Greek, Russian, Czech, Slovak, Polish, Slovene, Serbo-Croatian, Bulgarian, Old Church Slavonic, and Ancient Japanese—in short, of verse selected from a great many poetic traditions of the last thirteen centuries.

My listeners and readers almost always asked me, in various forms, the same five questions. First, why was I restricting my analyses to short poems ranging from couplets to a few dozen lines? There is no doubt that grammar is a vital factor in even the longest poems, but the laws that govern the organization of long poems differ on many points from those that rule the structure of short poems. As Edgar Allan Poe so subtly remarked, when one reaches the last line of a short poem, one clearly remembers the entire text, including the beginning. I have studied the grammar of long poems, but the interpretation of this structure requires a different, more complex presentation than the devices that allow us to disclose the structure of a short integral text. Thus, in my articles and courses I have refrained from passing too hastily to the analysis of longer texts, which are of a different order. Nonetheless, it goes without saying that the epic of Camoëns (1572), Pushkin's "Bronze Horseman," and the poem "May" by the Czech romantic Karel Hynek Mácha (1836), the same legacy of centuries that served as gratifying subject matter for my preliminary experiments, show a no less considerably refined grammatical structure as any short specimen of lyric poetry in the world.

An expert in and great admirer of the poetry of Alexander Pope (1688–1744), my Harvard colleague and friend Reuben Brower (1908–1975), tried to persuade me to analyze some of that poet's work, and in answer to my assertions that the "length was an obstacle," he proposed to furnish me with some integral fragments. I objected however that such attempts would too closely resemble the practice of those antiquarians who, in their hunger for gain, would cut large Italian frescoes up into small pieces: it would lead us to the error of looking at a fragment as if it were an entire poem.

The second type of question I was often asked pertained to manifestly poor poetry. I consider that in such poetry either there reigns a total grammatical chaos, or else the means of grammar are employed with hopeless banality.

The third question was as follows: is it possible from a study of the "grammar of poetry" to draw inferences about the personality of a poet, the style of a school, and the characteristic features of an epoch? The study of grammar no doubt places before the researcher tasks of considerable importance. Nonetheless, I think the first steps simply require analysis and interpretation of the text. Obviously the characteristic traits of one or another poet are manifesting themselves, the features that are common to his different works as well as the specific properties of his different genres, the different stages in his poetic development or even in his different poetic experiments. One can also begin to speak roughly of the common features of a poetic school or of a period. But I remain wary of premature generalizations.

First of all, we require a thorough study of the material, without premature historico-literary schemes or labels that foist upon the researcher an excessive degree of prejudgment. My first concern is to elaborate a sufficiently precise objective and fruitful technique for the purpose of revealing the grammatical contours of a text and highlighting its artistic effect. When one studies the grammatical profile of texts written at a given time, one immediately observes differences in the degree to which poets utilize grammatical figures and in their compositional procedures. The grammatical means are considerably richer and more important in function in the poetry of Khlebnikov and Osip Mandelshtam (1891–1938) than in that of their contemporary Majakovskij, where other means of language come to the fore. The *poètes maudits* such as Charles Baudelaire (1821–1867), the Pole Cyprian Norwid (1821–1883), and the Slovak Janko Král' (1822–1876), whose work marks an abrupt and direct passage from late Romanticism to Symbolism, reveal in their verse a marked penchant for grammatical figures.

Did I really think that a poet consciously organizes grammatical elements in his verse? This question, the fourth of the series, was repeatedly asked of me concerning the different procedures of poetic technique. It is true that a certain number of elements of the poetic art remain unconscious in the poet during the act of creation. However, the written and oral statements of poets, not to mention their early drafts, often show a real understanding of the different hidden methods of work on linguistic matter, especially when they work on grammatical material. This question is intimately linked with the doubts that have been expressed concerning the effects of grammatical juxtapositions and contrapositions on the person listening to or reading the verse: is he even aware of these subtleties?

Here it is necessary to distinguish between the experience of the formal components and their abstract cognition. The essential difference between these two modes of apprehension is seen with special clarity in music. In an audience which is intensely experiencing a piece of music, the percentage of those connoisseurs who know to what elements of composition they attend and who understand the secrets of their workings is quite small. One must also take account of the fact that there are differing degrees of awareness. Upon hearing two variants of the same stanza, one of which is endowed with a denser and more purposeful form than the other, many people can easily tell which is the more effective, but these same people are often incapable of answering the tricky technical question of why this is the case. What is more, as was noted by Edgar Allan Poe, many people find the experience of a work of art and the analysis of it into consciously experienced constituent parts mutually incompatible. In short, like many other aspects of a poem, grammatical structure generally affords the ordinary reader the possibility of an artistic perception, but produces neither the need nor the competence to effect a scientific analysis.

The fifth of the questions that are of concern to my readers and listeners deals with the objective awareness of a grammatical structure. To what extent is the choice of correspondences dictated by the material itself, and not by the subjective inclinations of the investigator? Is the picture of correspondences really something specific to poetry, or can one also find examples of this order in other kinds of texts, even newspaper articles? In fact, all attempts by these skeptics to find any example at all in newspapers or scientific journals of those constructions that recall the eloquent structuration of the grammar of poetry have ended in failure, and they strike us as totally helpless parodies of scientific work.

For my part, I have always attempted to maintain a maximum of objectivity when studying the grammatical aspects of poetic entities. It is really not difficult to see which grammatical categories contribute through their distribution to the artistic individualization of the parts, as well as to the integration of the whole poem, and which categories, on the contrary, remain passive. It is easy to verify statistically the likelihood and the precision of the choices one has made. When I study verse written in a language other than my own, I generally work with a specialist for whom it is the mother tongue. In any case, I am careful to verify my observations by consulting compatriots of the poet I am analyzing.

Despite their efforts, my critics have not been able to find a single important linguistic error in my examples of grammatical analysis. Verse presents all varieties of symmetrical construction: in addition to direct symmetry, we find extensive utilization of the so-called mirror symmetry and skillful antisymmetry; one finds a wide use of similar divisions in the rhythmical analysis of verse. The well-known forms of rhyme—plain, alternate, and enclosing (aabb, abab, abba)—find close typological parallels in grammatical figures. For example, in a poem with four stanzas, these figures may distinguish the first two stanzas from the last two, or the odd ones from the even, or finally the exterior two from the interior pair. The idea that it is possible to discover as many symmetrical categories as one wants is firmly contradicted by the concrete experience of analysis.

If a critic reads into studies of the grammar of poetry a secret intention on the part of the analyst to reduce poetry to a grammar, he is engaging in idle fantasy. In studying rhyme, no one went so far as to claim that poetry equals rhyme, just as one could never reduce poetry to a system of metaphors, or to a complex of stanzas, or to any other form and its various effects. Nonetheless, the study of rhymes, tropes, poetic rhythms, and the "figures of grammar" in Hopkins's terminology constitute many important objectives for the analysis of versification. The structure of verse was for a long time not subjected to rigorous analysis. More recently, attention has begun to be paid to the study of versification, and, in only the last few years, the grammatical analysis of poetry has also been placed on the order of the day. The determination of the principles of the rhythmic patterns in the work of a particular poet or poetic tradition is itself an interesting and useful undertaking, independent of the further question of the contributing role of these properties in the general "effect" of the poetic work. The same also holds for the study of grammatical figures.

To say to a student of structural linguistics that none
of these individual phenomena can be regarded as an
end in itself and that all the particular aspects of poetic
structure are interrelated so as to constitute a unique
whole—all that is like trying to break down doors that
are already open. However, from the point of view of
structural linguistics and poetics, it would be a serious
error to begin the analysis with a determination of the
"effects" of the poem, for making such a determination
without knowing the means in question can only lead to
naively impressionistic observations.

At present the linguist knows that one must not separate
questions of form and meaning. It would, however, be
no less of an error to decide on the signification of the
poetic totality without taking into account the constituent
elements of this totality. Explaining the grammatical
structure of the poem in relation to the architecture of
its stanzas is only the first step, to be followed by the
further fascinating question of the reasons for, or rather
the ends pursued by, the distribution of the chosen grammatical categories in the poetic whole. Nonetheless, in
my own practice I try as much as possible to sketch during
the initial grammatical analysis directions towards a semantic interpretation of the grammatical level that has
been discovered.

I regret having to say that the specific objections of my
critics plainly reveal insufficient familiarity with even
the most elementary questions involved in an analysis
of linguistic material. Thus, for example, Jonathan Culler,
in the chapter "Jakobson's Poetic Analyses" of his pre-
tentious book *Structuralist Poetics: Structuralism, Linguistics, and the Study of Literature* (London, 1975),

comments upon and disapproves of my approach to the last "Spleen" of Baudelaire. In the course of that analysis of Baudelaire's poem of five quatrains, I found a distinct contrast that opposed the three odd stanzas, all containing first-person pronouns, with the two even stanzas, where these forms were not to be found. Culler is at a loss to understand why I focused attention on the opposition of first-person forms to those in the third person, and he ascribes to me the fantastic idea that I was seeking to show, in the face of all facts to the contrary, the symmetrical distribution of even and odd stanzas. He does not know or does not want to know that the opposition between the speaking subject and the forms of the third person (in linguistic terms the "zero" person, the unmarked term) is one of the central oppositions among grammatical categories. It is precisely this opposition that underlies the traditional definition of lyric poetry as the poetry of the first person, and epic poetry as the poetry of the third.

This contrast of alternating stanzas is often used in poetry to show, as I observed in my analysis of the "Spleen," the "alternation of modes, one subjective, the other objective." In addition, by referring to the limited distribution of the first-person forms, one can easily determine not only the distribution of pronominal forms of the third person, but also the whole complex of the grammatical features of the even stanzas and the semantic composition of the entire poem. Culler has failed to notice that the two even stanzas, unlike the odd, contain reflexive pronouns, and that while the two types of stanzas, odd and even, follow the same order, the last line of each is distinguished by the obligatory presence of a personal pronoun.

Nor did he notice the equally important fact that, in the last line of each of the three odd stanzas, the form of the first person is immediately juxtaposed to the similar form of the third person, and that the first of the two forms is subordinated to the latter both syntactically and semantically. Thus we find the couples *il/nous* in the final line of the first stanza, *ses/nos* at the end of the third stanza, and *mon/son* in the last line of the fifth stanza.

The critic did not take into account the fact that the possessive forms of the first and third person appear each time in equal numbers: the plural forms *nos* and *ses* each appear once, and the singular forms *mon* and *son* each appear twice. Also, the three reflexive forms correspond to the three possessive forms—the three forms of the first person and the three forms of the third. Culler did not even notice the passage from the forms *nous* and *nos* to the more individualizing and subjectivizing *mon*, which appears for the first time in the final stanza where it occurs twice.

In discussing the contrast between odd and even stanzas, the critic should not disregard the contrast which, as I have indicated, separates the coordinating propositions that are typical of the odd stanzas on the one hand, and the multilevel hypotaxis that is characteristic of the even stanzas on the other.

Finally, Culler should not pass in silence over the semantic difference that diametrically opposes the movement "from the bottom to the top" of the even stanzas to the progression "from the top to the bottom" of the odd stanzas, especially since the entire metaphorical system of the "Spleen" is in fact based on this antithetical motion.

It is hard to understand why critics do their best to neglect grammatical figures in Baudelaire when the poet himself constantly referred to the "evocative magic" of grammatical structure, the expressive force of grammatical categories, and the poetic pertinence of such evident factors as "regularity and symmetry." That great expert on the work of Baudelaire, Théophile Gautier (1811–1872), devoted particular attention to the "trade secrets" hidden in this work and "invisible to outsiders."

All languages are based on a system of grammatical categories, and the meanings of these categories are characterized by the fact that they are obligatory for members of a given speech community, as Franz Boas and Edward Sapir, two inspired linguists of America, have pointed out. If we are speaking in a language in which singular and plural forms exist, then in discourse we are obliged to choose between the singular and the plural. If, on the other hand, we are speaking in a language that does not possess the forms of number, for example, some American Indian languages, we can express this distinction through lexical procedures, but we are not obliged to specify, for example, whether we are referring to one or to several ears of corn.

The network of grammatical categories determines the entire composition of our language, and the characteristic features of this network which remain shadowy in our everyday language become infinitely more expressive and more significant in poetry, as the example of grammatical parallelism concretely demonstrates. To see this it suffices to remember how vague and obscure the distinction of the grammatical genders of masculine and feminine is in ordinary language, while in poetry whenever this opposition is overtly expressed in the grammatical system of the language we notice its graphic and frequently decisive significance. These were the motives that inspired me to study the poetry of grammar and the grammar of poetry, and these inquiries, as they progressed, brought new light to questions in both poetry and grammar that had long remained obscure.

KP   I would like to add a few words in support of your statements on the role of grammar in poetry. If grammatical categories are obligatory for the speaker—and this is their unique and specific feature—then by virtue of this fact they constitute a particular kind of sign, a figure, a myth. It is for precisely this reason that their specific semantic potential is realized to such a high extent in poetic structure, in which, as you have indicated, it passes from a latent and hidden state to one that is manifest, straightforwardly significant, and symbolic.

It is not only such semantically delimited categories as gender or pronominal forms to which you have just referred that play a thematically dominant part in poetry: distinctions of grammatical case can do this as well. You have already pointed out the remarkable play of the direct and indirect cases in Pushkin's celebrated lyrical epistle "Ja vas ljubil" ("I loved you"). Let me add that the instrumental, that case which is so peculiar among those of the Russian system and of the Slavic system in general, acquires a particular function in Pasternak's "Sestra moja—žizn' " ("My sister—life"). Upon reading these lines of Pasternak's, one is struck by the distribution and frequency of the instrumental and by the variety of its numerous functions, ranging from the simple *instrumentalis modi* to the complex figure of comparison, the *simile*.

One discovers that this case, with its general signification indicating the peripheral role of the designated object, supports the whole complex of motifs of the poem: these motifs serve to highlight the vital role of elements that are normally seen as secondary or peripheral. If grammatical forms can become poetic figures, then grammar is far from being limited in its poetic function to an active role only in structures like rhyme. It acquires a role which is much more important and even universal.

13 SIMILARITY AND CONTIGUITY IN LANGUAGE AND LITERATURE, IN THE CINEMA, AND IN APHASIA

KP   We are coming now to one of the principal propositions of your theory: that the concepts of metaphor and metonymy are diametrically opposed phenomena. A century ago the Polish linguist Mikołaj Kruszewski observed the existence of these two poles in language, but it was only in your theory that they were treated for the first time as fundamental forces acting in language as well as in all forms of art. One is struck by the fact that in the course of your work on these problems you began by approaching them as problems in poetics and the theory of art, rather than in linguistics. You raise the issue for the first time, I believe, in "Futurism" (1919), one of your very first articles, and then return to it at the beginning of the thirties in such papers as "The Decline of the Cinema?" and the Czech and German versions of your "Notes on Pasternak's Prose." The issue arose again when you were in America preparing your essay on aphasia and child language, "Two Aspects of Language and Two Types of Aphasic Disturbances" (1956). Finally, in the synthetic article "Linguistics and Poetics," you raise the question again with reference to verbal art. A proper linguistic interpretation of metaphor and metonymy with appropriate physiological and neurological motivation appeared only during your American period, while your earlier approaches to this cluster of problems stood closer to semiotics. It would be interesting to learn the reasons for these contextual changes in your discoveries.

RJ   I came up against the problem of metaphor and metonymy very early in my scientific work. While still in high school, trying to get some grasp of the elementary concepts, I learned from our textbooks on-literary theory the routine definitions of these two terms and of other tropes and figures of speech. I quickly saw that the habitual formulae were quite sterile, and that it would be necessary to revise this entire outdated arsenal in order to transform it into a genuine scientific tool. I still firmly believe that this is a primary objective for the science of poetic language today, and not poetic language alone.

I found in my studies that reasonably sound principles of classical rhetoric had been smothered by legions of textbooks. When information theory returned the term and the concept of redundancy to linguistic and literary studies, it was a valuable acquisition. But it came to us from mathematics, and few among our coevals remembered its ancient source, the rhetoric of Quintilian. In the period during which poetry retreated from the essentially metaphoric slant of Symbolism, it was natural for it to turn to metonymy, the antithesis of metaphor. The fascinating experiments of the Cubist painters provided us with visual examples of the semantics of metonymy and especially of synecdoche, "the part for the whole," which is closely akin to metonymy.

It should be noted in passing that for us budding linguists semantics was our daily fare, while the problem of meaning was still unknown territory for the artists and writers who had grown up under the spell of external form. In 1919, the editorial board of the visual arts section of the Commissariat for Education in Moscow was discussing a project for an encyclopedia of the arts, and I was asked to join the discussion. When I proposed an article on the semantics of painting, Vasilij Kandinskij (1866–1944) had to explain to his perplexed colleagues what sort of beast "semantics" really was.

As a first-year graduate student in 1914, I naively decided to start my reading of Russian linguistics with the very first issue of the periodical *Russkij Filologičeskij Vestnik*, which was the Russian journal treating topics closest to those of linguistics. When I began studying its first issues, which appeared at the border of the 1870s and 1880s, I was immediately drawn to the unusual ideas of a young Polish scholar named Mikołaj Kruszewski, who had died at an early age and had been unjustly forgotten. Filip Fedorovich Fortunatov, the head of the Moscow linguistic school, had just died, and his offprints and pamphlets were being sold to the students. I thus came to own a remarkable article by Kruszewski on sound alternations (1881). This article, which had been written in German, had been turned down by the conservative editors of a German linguistic journal, and the author printed it at his own expense and sent a copy to Fortunatov. This is how the name of Kruszewski first entered my consciousness. (It is strange that he remains unknown to many linguists, and that his name is absent, for example, from the most recent one-volume edition of the *Polish Encyclopedia*.) Thus it was quite by accident that I became familiar with Kruszewski's attempt to extend and apply to language the theory of association by similarity and contiguity that he had found drafted by English thinkers.

At the beginning of 1920, Osip Maksimovich Brik (1888–1945), the collaborator of the Moscow Linguistic Circle who more than anyone else had the gift of formulating the issues of the times, took me by surprise with this pertinent remark: "We are all engaged in studying the artistic procedures of trends and works that are clearly oriented toward form. But what do you do about realism, which seems to be oriented toward values located outside of art?" This question set me to thinking, and, over a year later, when I was already in Prague, I answered it with the article, "On Realism in Art" (1921). Among the numerous interpretations of the very ambiguous term "realism," I observed that "realist literature" is often understood as narrative loaded with "images interconnected by contiguity. . . . This metonymic condensation supplements or even cancels the intrigue."

I was beginning to understand why scholars accorded so much attention to the metaphoric step based on association by similarity, and so little attention to the metonymic unfolding of the narration, which is based on association by contiguity. It is obvious that the former derives directly from the author's intention, while the latter seems more passive, more dependent upon the circumstances described than upon the creative will of the author. Yet construction through metonymy demands just as much artistic effort and refinement as does the linking of images by similarity.

During the early 1930s I had occasion to experience even more directly the intrinsic value of metonymic structures. The Ministry of Education had postponed my appointment as professor at Masaryk University in Brno because of the worsening economic crisis, and my close friend Vladislav Vančura (1891–1942), the great master of Czech prose, arranged for me to work on a screenplay. This gave me an opportunity to familiarize myself in detail with the methods of cinematographic art, which, in its essence, is metonymic in that it depends on an intense and varied exploitation of the play on contiguities. This vital aspect of the motion picture was particularly highlighted at that time by sporadic attempts at metaphoric presentations. For example, an image might dissolve into another that is not at all contiguous, but is similar: the contours of a forest of factory chimneys might be substituted for a dissolving view of the taiga. These lessons in the ABCs of cinematic techniques allowed me to appreciate the incomparable play of contiguities in the brilliant experiments of Buster Keaton (1895–1966), Charlie Chaplin (1889–1977), and Sergej Eisenstein (1898–1948), all of whom constantly broke the cliches of proximity in space and mechanical succession in time in order to reassemble the contiguous associations in original and unexpected ways. These innovators freed metonymy from its subjection to a merely mechanical association by contiguity and cast off the yoke of obvious similarity in metaphorical processes.

There was some affinity in this respect between these great filmmakers and Boris Pasternak (1890–1960), the virtuoso of metonymy in both poetry and poetic prose. It was no coincidence that my work passed directly from questions of cinematic art to complex problems in Pasternak's prose. In 1935, in my essay on his experimental prose, I wrote that the association by contiguity "becomes in Pasternak an effective instrument of the artist who proceeds to a redistribution of space and to modifications in the succession of time."

It was thus that I gradually gathered experience, once I had decided to compare metonymy and metaphor, those two radically different tropes that are both artistic transformations—the former of contiguity and the latter of similarity—and are differently articulated in the various forms of art. At the beginning of the fifties, when I was devoting my time to the linguistic aspects of various forms of aphasia (that is, to different impairments of language that result from cortical lesions), I discovered all of a sudden that the two principal types of aphasia were related in much the same way as were metaphor and metonymy. In one type, the patient experienced some degree of difficulty with associations by similarity; in the other, he experienced a comparable difficulty with associations by contiguity. At the same time, his fundamental linguistic operations suffered; in the first case selection (the paradigmatic axis), and in the second, combination (the syntagmatic axis). The first type of anomaly is primarily manifest in the process of perception, in the decoding activity of the receiver, and the second type in emission, in the encoding of the message by the speaker.

This reinterpretation of the traditional distinction between the so-called "sensory" and "motor" aphasia led me to all sorts of further research and conclusions. It provided the basis for a more articulated and precise classification of the linguistic syndromes of aphasia, and this new typology could readily be connected with the observations of neurologists on the relative topography of the cortical lesions that underlie the different kinds of aphasia. My research helped create a new interdisciplinary field, known today as neurolinguistics. As could have been expected, there were some backward neurologists who asserted that linguists had no business discussing the question of aphasia, and that neurologists had no reason to take linguistic information into account. Nonetheless, Aleksandr Luria (1902–1977), the first-rate specialist in aphasia who had worked intensely in the field for decades, gave recognition in a series of conclusive studies to the validity and fruitfulness of our attempts at classification. Some extremely recent experimental research done in Moscow on the relation between language and the brain has supported the cerebral topography of linguistic syndromes.

My linguistic studies of aphasia also permitted me to clarify some of the dichotomies essential to linguistic analysis—the reciprocal relation between the paradigmatic axis (selection) and the syntagmatic axis (combination) of language, and the relation between production and perception. Also, it seemed to me that the first observations of aphasic disturbances showed that the study of the multiple forms of aphasic disintegration of language could provide much information about the hierarchical structure of the system of language at its different levels. Indeed, the order of linguistic losses in the different types of aphasia is no less instructive than the order of acquisitions in the child for the determination of structural relations between the components of the linguistic system.

Finally, the analysis of the distribution of contiguities and similarities in the two aphasic syndromes continues to increase our comprehension of the opposite aspect, the maximal autonomous role played by similarities and contiguities in verbal art. It is no coincidence that the problem of literary similarities and contiguities that are promoted to the integral and intentional system of poetic language runs into frank incomprehension and perplexed objections on the part of critics. I had proposed that verse "projects the principle of equivalence from the axis of selection onto the axis of combination," and the critics took this thesis as an article of faith specific to a certain school of poetry and foreign to many other currents. They clearly did not understand the elementary fact that this thesis was nothing but an expanded tautology: it enters quite simply into the very definition of verse.

There is no verse without a system of repeated units, whatever the basic unit of that system may be: the syllable, equal to the syllable; the accent, equal to the accent; the quantitative measure, that is, the mora; even merely the unity of phrasal intonation. And where there is a repetition of units of the *signans*, there will inevitably arise the question of the reciprocal relations between the corresponding units of the *signatum*, as we have already observed in the example of rhyme, which necessarily belongs to both planes, the *signans* and the *signatum*. The moment when the lines or segments of lines corresponding to each other enter into a relation of similarity or contiguity, this relation—whether it be a similarity of two grammatical categories or of two units that are lexically close or only a syntactic narrative contiguity—is necessarily perceived. Correspondence by metrical position picks up and underscores the syntactic analogy of two subjects, or the morphological analogy of two nouns, or the lexical (and sometimes even phonic) analogy of two words, such as *père* and *mère* or *pater* and *mater*.

In contiguous metrical units, these relations are to be found at several levels and are intensified by an equivalence of position. Correspondence by metrical position picks up and underscores the syntactic contiguity of subject and predicate or the narrative contiguity of two words that treat two neighboring phenomena in space or time. Such are the contiguities reinforced by similar position in contiguous metrical units.

This heightened role of repetitiveness is essential to verse, yet this is not a mere mechanical repetition, for similarity necessarily includes some elements of dissimilarity. For instance, the words *père* and *mère*, which are similar in their phonic composition as well as in their meaning, are also distinctly different in phonic terms through the opposition between the presence and the absence of nasality in the first consonant, and through the fact that their signification, just as their common semantic basis (each represents a parent) contains the distinct contrast between masculine and feminine gender and sex. Finally, one should keep in mind that there is no insurmountable barrier between similarity and contiguity. The two are interconnected by context, as in the example, "My father and my mother went into town together." A critic may oppose modern poetry with its orientation toward "generalized similarity" to the poetry of François Malherbe (1555–1628), that "infamous enemy of all repetition," but one should acknowledge that this "hostility" is quite limited. The number of syllables, the position of the caesura, the pause at the end of the line— all are rigorously respected, and it is within this framework that all the possible similarities, contrasts, and contiguities of lexical units and grammatical forms are clearly manifest. For instance, the famous line, "Et rose elle a vécu ce que vivent les roses," presents a mirror symmetry of the two hemistichs: there is a repetition of the same substantive in different numbers and of the same verb in different persons and tenses, and there is an alternation of metaphorical and literal signification, not to mention the syntactic dissimilation of the repeated elements.

More and more works in poetics are considering this dualism of similarity and contiguity. It is now a matter of dealing with the concomitant questions of the relation between similarity and the various manifestations of contrast, and also between contiguity and degrees of distance other than immediate contiguity. One must—and this is most important—delimit and carefully consider the essential difference between the two aspects of contiguity: the exterior aspect (metonymy, in the proper sense of the word), and the interior aspect (synecdoche, which is close to metonymy yet essentially different). To show the hands of a shepherd in poetry or the cinema is not at all the same as showing his hut or his herd, a fact that is often insufficiently taken into account. The operation of synecdoche, with the part for the whole or the whole for the part, should be clearly distinguished from metonymic proximity, despite the undeniable kinship of these two contiguous tropes that both differ from the metaphorical relation founded on similarity. Like grammatical analysis in linguistics, poetics also must consistently take into account the similarity of metonymy and synecdoche and their difference from metaphor, in addition to, on the other hand, the difference between inner and outer contiguity, which marks the boundary between synecdoche and metonymy proper.

A linguistic study of aphasia closely linked to the theory of language in general and to poetic language in particular not only contributes to the classification of aphasic disorders, but also to the comprehension of the structure of language and even to the improvement of the methods of poetics. The next objective will be an attempt at a linguistic analysis of the language of schizophrenics. In all likelihood, the examination of the linguistic symptoms and syndromes of schizophrenia can support medical classification and diagnostics of the heterogeneous phenomena grouped together under the general label of schizophrenia. Such an undertaking would be a vast and difficult interdisciplinary program.

The great German poet Friedrich Hölderlin (1770–1843), who suffered for several decades from an extreme form of schizophrenia and toward the end of his life more or less lost the ability to communicate verbally with his surroundings, nonetheless continued until his death to write remarkable poems of an astonishing originality. In analyzing those poems, I tried once again to link the questions of poetics, speech pathology, and general speech communication. In this manner I succeeded in explicating the fundamental linguistic symptom of precisely that type of apparently widespread schizophrenia that afflicted Hölderlin. The gravely ill poet displayed a complete loss of the capacity and the desire for dialogical discourse; the most characteristic symptom of this loss was the total disappearance of shifters, particularly those of person and of grammatical tense. I am convinced that this preliminary exploration of the terrain must be followed by systematic linguistic investigation of the language of psychotics and of poetry, and that such comparative inquiries are particularly important for a global understanding of language as an instrument of mutual communication and of individual cognition.

14 THE BIOGRAPHY OF THE POET, POETRY AND MYTH

KP   The struggle for a new understanding of the role of biography in literary studies became one of the essential questions of the science at the beginning of the century. The OPOJAZ attacked this problem intensely, and its members did much to overcome the vulgar biographism of the old school. But at the same time they more or less eliminated biography as an object of scientific interest. One can discern this tendency clearly in Tynjanov and Eichenbaum, not to mention Shklovskij. Even Trubetzkoy, in his Viennese cycle of lectures on Dostoevskij (now available in book form), forcefully disavows any biographism in the study of the classic author. You yourself paid tribute to that tendency in your early study *Novejšaja russkaja poèzija* (*Recent Russian Poetry*). In it you formally reject any heterogeneous admixture, including biographism, in favor of a homogeneous method.

   Yet one should point out that at the beginning of the thirties you turned toward biography because of the lives of the two great poets, Pushkin and Majakovskij. After the latter's suicide in 1930, there appeared in Berlin your tribute, *O pokolenii, rastrativšem svoix poètov* (*On the Generation that Squandered its Poets*), which was published as a booklet along with an article by D. S. Mirskij (1890–1939) comparing the death of Majakovskii to the tragic end of Pushkin. It was clear that these two poets, living in a "cruel century," shared a common destiny, even though a hundred years separated them. Was it this comparison that subsequently led you to a preoccupation with biography, particularly that of Pushkin? (I am thinking of your work, "The Statue in Pushkin's Symbolism.") And it is not exactly a coincidence that it was precisely in the thirties, after Majakovskij's so tragic and mean-

ingful death, that you began to reflect on the life of the
poet, on his destiny, and not only on the symbolism and
rhythm of his verses, without living background.

RJ   In 1919, I was preparing with Khlebnikov a collection of
his work that, unfortunately, was never published. My
introduction to this collection, which initially bore the
title "Podstupy k Xlebnikovu" ("Approaches to Khlebnikov"), traced two of Khlebnikov's typical features: the
"laying bare of the device" to eliminate any motivation
for it, and the "realization of the device," its "projection
into artistic reality, the conversion of a poetic trope into
a poetic fact, a constituent of the plot," for instance, the
transformation of a metaphor into a metamorphosis. I had
attempted to show how "the word in the poetry of Khlebnikov loses its objectivity, then its internal form, and
finally even its external form," and tends toward maximally supraconscious language. It was only in the final
sentence of my essay that I passed from the verbal experiments of the author to the emotions that his own
experimentation had aroused in him. In the literary autobiography that Khlebnikov wrote apropos of my proposal
for his collected works, he described how writing the
supraconscious words of the dying Ekhnaten (the hero
of Khlebnikov's poetic narrative), "Mantch, mantch!," almost caused him physical pain: "I could not read them.
I saw lightning between me and them. Now they are
nothing to me, I myself don't know why." It was with
this allusion to the emotions of the poet that I concluded
my essay.

    My initial thesis, that we perceive every fact of poetic
language in the present by necessarily confronting it with
the "poetic tendency that underlies the phenomena in

question," was of course supported by this same autobiographical acknowledgment by Khlebnikov: "When I
observed that older lines suddenly faded, when their hidden content became the present day, I understood that
the home of creation was the future. It is from there that
the winds of the gods of the word blow." Poets have made
this confession from time immemorial; one has only to
recall the words of Percy Bysshe Shelley (1792–1822) in
his *Defense of Poetry*: "Poets are . . . the mirrors of the
gigantic shadows which futurity casts upon the present;
the words which express what they understand not. . . ."
This slogan was particularly near to Futurism, which was
directed in its entire pathos toward the future, and therefore the words of the Russian poet, so pregnant with the
future, kept his past life hidden from us at that time. But
in 1930, after we lost Majakovskij, I noted the following:
"We strained toward the future too impetuously and av-
idly to leave any past behind us. The time was out of
joint. We lived too much for the future, thought about
it, believed in it; the news of the day—sufficient unto
itself—no longer existed for us. We lost a sense of the
present. . . . All we had were compelling songs of the
future; and suddenly these songs are no longer part of
the dynamic of history, but have been transformed into
historico-literary facts."

In these circumstances the question of our loss and of
the lost poet forced itself upon us. Majakovskij had more
than once stated that for him, the poet's realism did not
consist of picking up the crumbs of the past, nor of re-
flecting the present, but rather of creatively anticipating
the future. And we did indeed discover that the poet had
recounted his destiny in advance, had foreseen his fateful

end, and had even precisely guessed and described all
the absurd and unpitying reactions of his contemporaries
to his "unexpected," but timely, death. And what was
even more surprising and sinister, the readers of Majakovskij did not see, or did not want to see, the detailed
prophecies contained in his verse that were realized to
the letter. When the poet was no longer, they carried out
with the utmost zeal the parodying roles that the biting
satire of the poet had dictated to them in advance.

Throughout the course of his poems, Majakovskij had
sketched out the monolithic myth of the poet, a zealot
in the name of the revolution of the spirit, a martyr condemned to cruel and hostile incomprehension and rejection: "The massacre was over. . . . Alone above the
Kremlin, the shreds of the poet waved in the wind like
a red flag." When this myth entered the sphere of life,
it became impossible to trace a limit between the poetic
mythology and the curriculum vitae of the author without
committing terrible forgeries. The testament of Majakovskij found its full justification: in the authentic life
of the poet, only that which "ferments into a word" is
meaningful.

Yes, this is the important issue, but often critics are
either incapable of fully comprehending it or even indifferent to its perception. In an unfinished poem first
entitled the "Fourth" and subsequently the "Fifth International," on which Majakovskij worked with passion
and perseverance from 1921 to 1922, the poet tells how
in the "future communist fullness" the revolution of the
spirit, manifestly and of necessity, will "spring forth from
time" according to the expression of the poet: "I will do
it myself, for apart from me there is no one to reflect

upon it." It is thus that the essential duty of the "communards-Futurists" is defined by Majakovskij in this poem, which, in the words of the poet, was easy to envision but difficult to write down. In the drafts of the poem that he had written at the beginning of 1922, Majakovskij outlines the dialogue with Lenin that history has predestined him for in the cosmic future; Lenin brushes aside this importunate newcomer with the pretext that he had "never met him at the SOVNARKOM (Council of Peoples' Commissars)," to which Majakovskij firmly replies: "Do not wave me away. Today *I* am president of the SOVNARKOM." According to the poet's account of this future verbal duel, Lenin is convinced that Majakovskij is "speaking nonsense—he should be whipped!" There is no doubt that this is a paraphrase of Lenin's note dated May 6, 1921, a note that Majakovskij knew and detested. In it Lenin voices his bitter opposition to the agreement made by Lunacharskij, the Commissar of Education, to publish Majakovskij's poem "150 000 000." The high point of this poem, written in 1919–1920, is the following: "My poem is written neither for Trotskij nor for Lenin. I glorify the combat of the millions. I see the millions, and it is of them that I sing." In his categorical pronouncement, Lenin characterizes that powerful poem as "nonsense, stupidity, and pretentiousness," and he puts forth a proposition of his own: "Lunacharskij should be whipped for his Futurism."

The preliminary drafts for the "Fifth International" are full of poetic images of Lenin slowly lifting his "enormous eyelids" and "opening his leaden lips." These images deliberately tie the figure of Lenin, sketched out for the poem yet to come, to Vij, that demonic being from Gogol's story of the same name, who appears several times in Majakovskij's poetry. Vij was a creature with an iron face who was incapable of seeing anything from behind his long eyelids that drooped down to the ground. Majakovskij, we recall, had promised to the Komsomols (the communist youth) in his poem of 1923, "O novoj religii" ("On the new religion"), that from that time on "the witches and the Vijs would no longer rave against the mind." In 1921, Lenin called upon M. N. Pokrovskij: "I entreat you immediately to support me in the struggle against Futurism, etc. It must be cut short." The draft of the "Fifth International" answered gallantly:

No enclosure will succeed in suffocating me
Even if you are multiplied fourfold, wall of the
    Kremlin,
I will take flight from the pavement and I will
    inscribe myself in the ear of the rebels
With the cry of my outraged song.

It is worth noting that the images of the "Fifth International" return in the poem of 1924–1925 in which Majakovskij glorifies Lenin upon his death, but in the conditional mood; they were suppressed during the "cult of personality":

If he had been majestic and divine,
I would not have held back my rage,
I would have blocked the path of the processions,
and laid across the adorations and the crowds
I would have found the words of a thundering
    malediction
and, while my cry and I were crushed underfoot,
I would have sent my blasphemies to the skies,

in the form of bombs, I would have cried "Down!"
to the Kremlin.

We should observe that Majakovskij had been describing the physicist Albert Einstein as a heroic fighter for
the Fifth International since the early 1920s, despite
Lenin's warnings that Einstein and his theory, in their
increasing popularity, posed dangers to the claims of the
orthodoxy. The enthusiasm for the "futurist brain of Einstein" entered into the play *Banja* (*Bathhouse*), which
Majakovskij was writing shortly before his death, in the
monologue of the inventor of the miraculous time ma-
chine that "broke down the door of the future."

Majakovskij was the principal figure, in both a positive
and a negative light, in the autobiographical essays of
Boris Pasternak. Pasternak had been in turn attracted and
repelled, and then finally violently repelled, by this hero,
which resulted in his contradictory account of his attitude
toward Majakovskij over time. So it is not without reason
that one of Pasternak's most remarkable works, the lyrical
prose of his autobiography *Oxrannaja Gramota* (*Safe
Conduct*), ends with these words on Majakovskij, who
had just died: "He was spoiled from childhood by the
future, which had been given to him at a young age,
without requiring him to make any great effort." Such
had been, in the eyes of the living poet, the life "now
passed once and for all" of this deceased friend whom
he later was to see as his life enemy. *Safe Conduct* is a
skein of metonymic contradictions, of tangled spatial,
temporal, and causal ties, which hide behind a sequence
of reversals the true face of the author and hero of the
book. I sent Pasternak my article on his metonymical
prose, *Safe Conduct* in particular, and he answered with

a long autobiographical letter in which he used that meaningful and extremely metonymic term "displaced"; he referred to his increasing conviction that the personal life of the poet, and not only a poet, and not only now, and not only in our land, is displaced.

During the thirties, my last decade in Czechoslovakia, I became an enthusiast of Czech poetry, in particular the works of two romantics, Karel Hynek Mácha and Karel Jaromir Erben (1811–1870), both of whom, although relatively unknown outside Czech circles, were lyric poets of world stature. I experienced very intensely the sumptuous expansion, also unknown abroad, of avant-garde Czech poetry between the wars. The young Czech poets and painters made me a member of their circle, and I became very close to some of them. Once again, as in my youth in Moscow, the same experience was repeated: we proved to be closer to one another through our dreams and our goals than we were to the Prague scholars of our age. Vítězslav Nezval (1900–1958), the brilliant poet of our generation, referred to this in his poems. I would not want to forget a great painter of that group, Joseph Šíma (1891–1971), who wandered during those years between Paris and Prague, and who noted in his personal journal of the twenties my discussions with him on my great preoccupations at that time, the binary structure of linguistic signs and the semantics of parallelism. He claimed that these discussions were reflected in his own research on painting.

My intimate knowledge of Czech artistic circles allowed me to comprehend fully the force of Czech literary art from the Middle Ages to today, and it was this connection that prompted me to undertake the gratifying task of a decisive revision of the Czech romantics from a new standpoint. The question naturally arose of the internal relation between life and creativity. I also saw that it was necessary to oppose this question to the vulgar conception of poetic fiction as a mechanical superstructure on reality, as well as to the equally vulgar dogma that I call "antibiographism," which rejects any relation between art and its personal and social background. I attempted to demonstrate, using the example of Mácha's verses, diaries, and letters, that there is no precise delineation between biographical "truth" and poetic "fiction." The diverse and contradictory versions of the same myth are capriciously distributed throughout his published verse, his correspondence with his friends, and his personal diary, which is in part in "cipher." It would be impossible to deny to any of these versions an organic link between poetic work and daily chronicle.

The problem of invariance and variations, which runs through almost all of my works on the phonic and grammatical structure of language and on the laws of verse, appeared here in another dimension. According to the banal formula, the output of many authors is permeated with thematic unities that show through the temporal sequence of the diverse motifs of the author's creation. It was necessary to grasp the essence of this unity and give it a convincing interpretation in its relation to the variable motifs. Behind the fancifully mutable symbolics of the poet stood the invariant of the myth of the poet: a myth that aimed at the maximally personal identification of the conventional literary *I* with the "passport person" of the author, or, on the contrary, at the creation of a myth that seeks its justification in traditional mythology. The poetics of Mácha eloquently displayed the first tendency, while the ballads of Erben exemplified the latter, which was characteristic of the conservative wing of the romantic pursuit.

Pasternak, in the letter mentioned above, stated that reading his own poems and prose in Czech, a language at once close to and different from Russian, had played an essential role in his work. His own writings, having become dead letters, already weighed down upon him, but when he read them in a new version that at the same time was similar in language, he derived inspiration for renewal of his work. As for myself, while editing the Pushkin translations I had the experience of reading the Czech reshaping of those Russian lines I had known from childhood, and I suddenly discovered features that neither I nor anyone else had noticed in the original. The similarity in form even of certain titles—"Kamennyj gost' " ("The stone guest"), "Mednyj Vsadnik" ("The Bronze Horseman"), "Zolotoj Petušok" ("The Golden Cockerel")—provided me with a key for analyzing the communality of plot and similarity of detail in these three works that Pushkin had written at the same distant estate, but in three different years. They also presented striking differences in genre: drama, epic poem, and fairy tale. It became immediately clear that all three were variations on Pushkin's myth of the destructive statue. This myth found close parallels in Pushkin's treatment of sculpture and sculptural semantics, particularly in his interpretation of the dramatic opposition between movement and immobility. I found it just as instructive to study the theme of the demonic statue in the context of Pushkin's letters and biographic events. The question raised by all this was an embarrassing one: how could it have escaped the attention of his commentators? How did it come to seem that Pushkin was indifferent to the plastic arts? There was only one unequivocal answer: the myth of the poet is so integral and so organically merged with its separate variants that it is just as difficult to separate the heroes of the titles of these three works from the myth as it is to identify them with three real statues.

While the myth may have an autonomous existence in the work of the poet, this in no way precludes research into the historical premises of this myth and its different versions in the writer's work. One cannot deny, for example, that there is some tie between Pushkin's search for a way to adapt himself to Nicholas's Petersburg and the poet's myth of the punishment of the statue. What is more, the role of the future in the poetic work—so clearly understood by Khlebnikov when he spoke of the future as the realm of creation, and by Majakovskij when he defined artistic realism—sometimes illuminates the prophetic signification of the myth which a poet creates of his own destiny. The examples of Pushkin and Majakovskij are in no way unique. As for Pushkin, the dreams he attributes to the unattractive hero of "The Bronze Horseman" of a reassuring marriage, cabbage soup, and the prestige of the small landowner coincide almost word for word with the confessions he makes in his own name in the chapter on the journeys of Eugene Onegin. The tragic antinomy, "my heart asks for peace," continually evolves as it passes from the victims of the destructive statue to the lyric epistles that Pushkin addressed to his wife, from the poetic agony to the agony of the duelling poet.

The semiotic problems of the interrelations between verbal art and plastic art, between the similarity and the contiguity of sculptures, as well as the question of the interpretation of the statue as an idol in the Russian spiritual tradition, engendered new ideas about the semiotics of the arts and the links between semiotics and mythology. My research on the relations between myth and the historical background of the poetic work subsequently led me to the Russian oral heroic epic.

A few hours before the invasion of Czechoslovakia by the German army, I sent my article "Sobaka Kalin Car' " ("Kalin Tsar, the Dog") to Professor Oldřich Hujer (1880–1942), the editor of the Prague review *Slavia*, with the proposal that he publish it under the pseudonym Olaf Jansen if necessary. The article was dedicated to "The radiant memory of Vsevolod Fedorovich Miller," who had headed the historical school of the study of the Russian epic and had directed the Lazarev Institute during my first years of study there. I believe I succeeded in establishing in this article that the mysterious tsar Kalin, usually referred to in the *byliny* by the epithet "dog," had his historical model in the Tatar aggressor and enemy of Kievan Russia who was known by the totemic name "Nogai," which goes back to the Mongol word for dog. This individual appears in Muslim sources with the title of *melik* ("tsar"), and with the Turkish epithet *jasu* ("large"), which is a synonym for the rarer and less polite Turkish adjective *kalyn* ("fat"). In the Russian *bylina*, this Turkish epithet was transformed in translation into the name Kalin, while the proper name Nogai was turned into an ironic epithet. The principal theme of my article concerned the question of the fusion of historical facts with the requirements of the epic tradition.

The problem of the plurality of levels and, at the same time, the artistic integrity of the Russian epic was addressed in a far more detailed fashion ten years later in New York, in The Vseslav Epos, a piece of work I carried out with the historian of the Slavic world, Marc Szeftel. This work was the result of our collective research on the Igor Tale, a monument of Russian literature dating from the turn of the twelfth and thirteenth centuries, whose subject is the eleventh-century magic prince of the town of Polotsk. This masterpiece of pre-Tatar Russian history, and the echoes of this tale from the Tatar era, required from me and my colleagues Henri Grégoire (1881–1964), Marc Szeftel, and, for the Tatar era, Dean Worth, the most painstaking, rigorous, and exhaustive textual criticism, including careful attention to legendary tradition, both oral and written. After this monograph on the Igor Tale, I undertook a digression: a study in collaboration with the Serbian philologist Gojko Ružičić (1894–1974) on the essential effects of this tradition, which apparently dates back to the time of Common Slavic in the epic cycles of the southern Slavs, cycles which were generally assigned to a local despot of the fifteenth century nicknamed Zmaj Ognjeni Vuk.

These two studies led to a justification of the three classical approaches that could be advanced for the epic heritage of the Slavs: one in the mythological substratum, another through literary borrowings, and the third in historical reflections. But all these elements must be minutely determined, and they should be treated as the harmonious parts of an artistic whole rather than disparate entities mechanically joined together. From the fascinating question of the transformation of a myth into an epic, the path led to the systematic presentation of tasks for a comparative reconstruction of Slavic mythology, and then to a wide utilization of this mythology in the reconstruction of common Indo-European mythology. My courses at Harvard during the sixties were devoted to these issues, as were my reports (subsequently published) to the anthropological congress in Moscow in 1964, and the congress of Slavists in Prague in 1968. Nonetheless, the greater part of my material and of my conclusions still await definitive elaboration and publication.

I based these studies on the following methodological principles: in place of the general skepticism that denied *a priori* that medieval writings and contemporary folklore could contain vestiges and authentic evidence of Slavic mythology, I substituted the systematic use of the sources at our disposal. I aimed at the reconstruction, insofar as possible, of pre-Christian Slavic beliefs. Certain mythological names were attested to in the written and oral heritage, and there were fragmentary indications of their contexts and functions to be found as well. This fact called for the comparative analysis of the Slavic repertory of analogous names, and even of vestigial terms existing in ethics and religious rites. This entire complex of terms and proper names had to be meticulously compared to the similar heritages of the other Indo-European branches. In addition, we had to separate the elements that would lead to the understanding of a common prehistoric genesis from those phenomena of intertribal cultural diffusion. One is always discovering more examples of the same phenomenon in the history of the spiritual relations between the Slavs and the Indo-Iranian world, especially its Iranian segment. With the evolution of research in the domain of comparative mythology, one increasingly observes that some Slavic vestiges are more archaic than the monuments of ancient Germanic, or Vedic, mythology which, although much older, have been subject to literary reshaping.

The following question arises: what is the common denominator of all these preoccupations with myth, from the cycle of Pushkin's work on the demonic statue, to the mythological background of the Russian folk epic, and finally to the attempts to apply the methods of comparative linguistics to Common Slavic and Indo-European mythology? The chief conclusions remind one to some extent of the fascinating debates among contemporary anthropologists on the character, extent, and range of application of the idea of myth. These conclusions can roughly be paraphrased in the following way: poetry and myth are two closely linked forces that are at the same time quite contradictory. The collision between these two elementary forces lies in the fact that poetry is oriented toward variation, while myth aims at invariance. For me, this communality and difference are connected with a number of mutual relations between poetry and myth, namely the possibility of a deeply individual poetic myth that is hidden behind patent variants: the rulers of destiny—the statues in Pushkin's poems, for example; or the conversion of the ethnic myth into the profoundly personal ballads of Erben; or even the projection of myth into history, for example, the oral epic of the magic prince; and finally the destinies of the Indo-European mythological system, which is transformed into individualized literary works, or still lives in a few belated folk echoes.

All of this is but a first blueprint, a sketch for future inquiries on this fascinating theme of mythic and poetic creation.

KP In your treatment of poetic mythology, you show the vital link between this and the autobiographies of Majakovskij and Pasternak. Despite their apparent dissimilarities, these two texts have much in common. Their common method of treating all that is essential or futile in the life and the biography of the poet is particularly significant. For both of them, only that which is "fermented into words" is essential. But there is one particular aspect that directly concerns your approach to biographical facts and to symbolic facts. The biographies of both poets, especially Pasternak's *Safe Conduct*, show that so-called real facts do not exist for the poet. Each detail of life is instantaneously transformed into a symbolic element and only in this form is it linked to the poet. Here lies a precise parallel to your study of the creation of myth in Pushkin; in it you noted in the "real" biography of the poet an entire series of symbolic phenomena available to him and which were at least as important, if not more so, as real events. Here the boundary between poetic myth and ordinary life is effaced. This was the reason for Pasternak to say that "only the hero deserved a true biography." The life of the poet cannot be imagined in this manner, for "the poet gives to his whole life such a voluntarily steeply-curved incline that it is not possible for it to exist in the direct vertical line of biography." If one attempts to force the biography of the poet along this vertical line, "one would be reduced to composing it out of insignificant data."

15 SEMIOTICS

KP   It would seem that semiotics, which encompasses the science of language as a system of signs, treats that science in a synthetic manner. Therefore, this will be the theme of my last question. But it is a difficult one to formulate, because you have in fact studied literary and artistic phenomena as signs throughout your scientific activity in all domains of language and art. One would think that this would have exhausted questions of semiotics. Nonetheless, you have devoted a certain number of works to semiotics as a particular discipline and to the history of that discipline: for example, "Language in Relation to Other Communication Systems," "Linguistics in its Relation to Other Sciences," and "A Glance at the Development of Semiotics." These studies were all composed recently, beginning at the end of the sixties.

    There is a host of multiplying questions centered around the problem of the reciprocal relations between linguistics and semiotics: can one say that semiotics encompasses all linguistic research? Can one consider semiotics as simply a balance sheet? Why has semiotics become such a popular, even fashionable, discipline in the last ten years? Does this inflation of semiotic questions run the risk of reducing their scientific value? What are the limits and the perspectives of semiotics?

RJ   Just before the outbreak of the First World War, I had a number of impassioned discussions with the young painters in Moscow on the problem of the ties and the differences between the diverse forms of art, particularly between the pictorial sign as an element of painting and the verbal sign as an element of language, and the conversion of these two types of signs into abstract painting and supraconscious poetry.

The themes and terminology of the sign had attracted these young explorers for some time. When we became acquainted with the thoughts of Saussure, the question of the science of signs (semiology, as Saussure called it in his fight for a new discipline) immediately entered into our conversations and our projects and was discussed in the meetings of the then recently formed Prague Linguistic Circle. The esthetician Jan Mukařovský (1891–1975), in particular, advanced in this direction at that critical turning point of the thirties and forties. Of all the semiotic types and all the forms of art, language and verbal art remained the fundamental and favored topics of the Circle between the wars.

For my part, I began to analyze the problem of the place of language in culture and its significance in the complex of other systems of signs, all in the course of my research on the Slavic and especially Czech Middle Ages, which opened up intriguing perspectives. Until that time, the domain had never been studied closely enough in all its aspects, nor been approached and interpreted as it should have been. The so-called Moravian Mission was probably a decisive event, not only for Czech medieval history, but for Slavic history in general. It was conducted during the second half of the ninth century by Constantine-Cyril (827–869) of Thessalonica, a remarkable linguist and thinker who was first a student and later a scholar at the university at Constantinople, then the only university in Europe. The major contribution of Constantine, and Methodius (?–885), his older brother and active collaborator, not only to Slavic culture but also to the traditions and existence of the Slavs was their translations of the Scriptures and ecclesiastical texts, into the newly formed

Slavic literary language. The missionary brothers and their Slavic disciples carried on a painful struggle for the Slavic church, using as their emblem a few ideological slogans that are extremely interesting when subjected to a semiotic interpretation. Instead of the Saussurian term semiology, I use the now generally accepted term semiotics, which was first proposed by John Locke (1632–1704) and then later taken up by Charles Sanders Peirce. Peirce devoted his life to founding this science and to tracing its first, vast program, which even today answers the needs of modern thought.

A thousand years before Peirce proposed his visionary theses to the American Academy of Sciences, Constantine composed in Slavic verses the remarkable prologue (*proglas*) to his translation of the four gospels. Through an eloquent chain of metaphors, he looks for and finds the summit of human essence in the word that is heard, read, and understood:

Then hear now with your own mind,
Since you have learned to hear, Slavic people,
Hear the Word, for it came from God,
The Word nourishing human souls,
The Word strengthening heart and mind,
The Word preparing all to know God.
As without light there can be no joy—
For while the eye sees all of God's creation,
Still what is seen without light lacks beauty—
So it is with every soul lacking letters,
Ignorant of God's law,
The sacred law of the Scriptures,
The law that reveals God's paradise.
For what ear not hearing

The sound of thunder, can fear God?
Or how can nostrils which smell no flower
Sense the Divine miracle?
And the mouth which tastes no sweetness
Makes man like stone;
Even more, the soul lacking letters
Grows dead in human beings.
Thus, considering all this, brethren,
We speak fitting counsel
Which will divide men
From brutish existence and desire,
So that you will not have intellect without
    intelligence,
Hearing the Word in a foreign tongue,
As if you heard only the voice of a copper bell.

In this manner, Constantine asserts the right and the
duty of every people to linguistic self-determination; he
takes the Old Testament symbol of the confusion of
tongues at Babel as the punishment of God and opposes
to it the New Testament symbol of the miracle of Pen-
tecost with the descent of the Holy Spirit, which, by its
gift of language, transfigures the plurality of human languages into a manifestation of divine Grace. The Slavic
language, according to the doctrine of the Moravian Mission, had the right to participate in the mystery of the
Eucharist, which in the Middle Ages was the supreme
spiritual value and from which automatically followed
the right to a deciding role for all social values.

In the Slavic verses of Constantine there has been preserved for us the prayer pronounced by the priest before
the transubstantiation of bread and wine into the body
and blood of Christ. The Hussites referred to this Old

Church Slavonic precedent at the time of the revolutionary struggle for the people's self-determination, and even the Czech scholar Bohuslav Balbín (1621–1688), in the climate of the triumphant Counterreformation, exalted the Slavic language of the prayer of the Eucharist as the greatest right given to the people, for the words pronounced by the priest are an even greater miracle than that of the creation of the material world by God.

Constantine-Cyril was closely acquainted not only with the link between these two symbolic systems, the word and the rite, but also with the tie that binds the words and rites of the church to visual art. It is characteristic that the *Vita* of Cyril in Old Slavonic praises him for his moral victory in defending icons to the high priest of the iconoclasts. This tie between the ritual signs of the ceremony, the verbal signs of the mother tongue, and the iconographic signs in the historical struggle for a language to be used in the divine service, and therefore for the entire culture, which would be understandable to everyone, and thus for equality for every person and every people, has been insufficiently appreciated by the skeptical school of medievalists. The dispute with this school still provides scholarship with new, unexpected proofs of the breadth and depth of the Moravian exploit. This eloquent example of the supreme role of language in its multiple and creative relations with other systems of signs gives us a lesson in general semiotics, and calls for the inclusion of linguistics in the ensemble of vaster cultural and sociopolitical problems.

It seems to me that the determination of the sociocultural framework of language and the historical work that this entails is a necessary complement to the versatile analysis of the internal structure of language. For my part, I would have preferred to speak not of a complement but rather of two clearly correlative planes of analysis, without subordinating one to the other a priori. The refusal to recognize the presence and importance of these two planes, which are at once autonomous and correlative, is as obtuse as to deny the indisputable truth that language is an integral part of an entire complex of semiotic systems. No matter what may be the hierarchical relation between these systems, particularly between language and the other spheres of signs, we must now clearly undertake the comparative study of language and all the other groups of signs, a study that has been planned over the course of centuries by a whole succession of thinkers. One would have to be myopic not to agree.

Mixed in with the many essays of value that contribute to the constitution of such a science, there of course occur articles of a dilettantish and superficial character. But the argument applies against these frivolous manifestations themselves, and not against the discipline whose terminology and slogans the authors of these vain efforts imprudently borrow. There has never been a science, or a new stage in the history of the different sciences, that did not in the beginning have its false creators and parasites who followed fashion and the seduction of novelty. This has been the case with all the new "schools" of linguistics, at least from the Enlightenment to the present day. In addition, every new step is characterized by purely theoretical disputes over the desirable limits of the new science.

As for the question of which genres of signs enter into the frame of semiotics, there can be only one answer: if semiotics is the science of signs, as the etymology of the word suggests, then it does not exclude any sign. If, in the variety of the systems of signs, one discovers systems that differ from others by their specific properties, one can place them in a special class without removing them from the general science of signs. The number and range of concrete objectives that present themselves to semiotics argue for their systematic elaboration around the world. However, one should reject all the unsuitable efforts of sectarians who seek to narrow this vast and varied work by introducing into it a parochial spirit.

Afterword

In his recent work, the farsighted Russian linguist Vjacheslav Vsevolodovich Ivanov has convincingly demonstrated the extent to which modern science and the theater arts are connected in ways that are both strong and subtle (V. V. Ivanov, "Sovremennaja nauka i teatr," *Teatr* No. 8, 1977) ("Contemporary Science and Theater"). The important fact here is not a direct causal link but the feedback system. The theater owes a great deal to modern physics, neurology, and psychology, but these disciplines are in turn indebted to the theater. The most active role for these disciplines is played by the theory of movement, which was already articulated by Heinrich Kleist (1777–1811) in 1810, and which, through the theater of E. G. Craig (1872–1966) and of Vsevolod Emil'evich Meyerhold (1874–1942) and the cinema of Eisenstein, influenced contemporary biomechanics and had a profound effect on the formation of the disciplines in question. What is signaled here is the complex nature of the relations between the different domains, as well as the unexpected part played by art in the lives of men.

Precisely this type of dialectic of feedback is applicable to the works and the very mind of Roman Jakobson. When he examines his own writing, he always emphasizes the link that ties his innovative tendencies to recent experimental art. It is in the "Retrospect" to the first volume of his *Selected Writings* (1962; second edition 1971) that he poses this question, apparently for the first time, with particular conciseness:

Perhaps the strongest impulse toward a shift in the approach to language and linguistics, however, was—for me, at least—the turbulent artistic movement of the early twentieth century. The great men of art born in the 1880s—Picasso (1881–1973), Joyce (1882–1941), Braque

(1882 –1963), Stravinsky (1882 –1971), Khlebnikov (1885–1922), Le Corbusier (1887–1965)—were able to complete a thorough and comprehensive schooling in one of the most placid spans of world history. . . . The extraordinary capacity of these discoverers to overcome again and again the faded habits of their own yesterdays, together with an unprecedented gift for seizing and shaping anew every older tradition or foreign model without sacrificing the stamp of their own permanent individuality in the amazing polyphony of ever new creations, is intimately allied to their unique feeling for the dialectic tension between the parts and the uniting whole, and between the conjugated parts, primarily between the two aspects of any artistic sign, its *signans* and its *signatum*. . . . Those of us who were concerned with language learned to apply the principle of relativity in linguistic operations; we were consistently drawn in this direction by the spectacular development of modern physics and by the pictorial theory and practice of cubism, where everything "is based on relationship" and interaction between parts and wholes, between color and shape, between the representation and the represented.

We are faced here, once again, with the phenomenon of the close interdependence of art and the exact sciences, and of the influence that the one as much as the other has had on the new linguistics. Jakobson's discoveries in the domain of linguistics returned to art for their creative impulse, and his entire spiritual orientation must be viewed as both the result and the corrective of the art and the science of the avant-garde. Jakobson's very first works on the new art posed the problem of the parallelism between the character of this art and of social life, as well as science. This was the case in the young scholar's article on Dada, written in Prague for the Moscow journal *Vestnik teatra* (1921), in which he tied the question of contemporary Russia, where "there is no longer any such thing as an everyday routine," to the theory of relativity,

which had come to replace "the science of the thousand-
and-one examples, so typical in those days ruled by the
formula 'so it was, so it will be,' where tomorrow has
pledged to be like today, and an honest man has his *chez
soi*." He studied the theory of relativity even earlier, in
Moscow in the article "Futurism" (1919), in which he
compared the evolution of the new painting, with its
decomposition of light and color and then even of the
object, to the evolution of the exact sciences and
particularly to the physics of Einstein.

How do we conceive of time? As something continuous
which passes at a constant and eternal speed. Time is
the same throughout the universe; there do not exist,
and apparently there cannot exist, two times which would
flow at different speeds in two different places in the
universe. The same holds true of our notion of the 'simultaneity' of two events, the 'before' and the 'after,' as
if these three concepts, so elementary, within the grasp
of a child, had an identical meaning for everyone every-
where. . . . Time becomes a part of all three dimensions.
We cannot determine the geometrical form of a body in
movement in relation to us. We always define its kinetic
form. Thus, our spatial dimensions in fact do not exist
in a three-dimensional diversity but in a four-dimensional
one.

These thoughts were held by O. D. Khvol'son and
N. A. Umov, Russian physicists of that time, and were
often quoted by the young linguist, fascinated as he was
by the paintings of the Futurists. These same thoughts
underlie his linguistic research and remain alive
throughout all of his work. This is especially true of his
interest in the roles of space and time in the evolution
and different functions of language. These themes pass
like a leitmotif throughout our dialogues.

Another noteworthy feature of Roman Jakobson's creative genius is the constancy of his scientific interests. He never turns his back on the passions of his youth: there is no flight into another domain, only a consistent elaboration of the same fundamental premises with an ever wider inclusion of more and more vast material. This is the reason that the linguist Grigorij Osipovich Vinokur (1896–1947), in his notes on Jakobson's work, underscores his "conservatism, in the face of all the revolutionary spirit of his discoveries, for he constantly remains faithful to the interests and principles of his early youth."

We can add yet one more particularity of the protagonist of *Dialogues*, one which Morris Halle points out in his article for the *International Encyclopedia of the Social Sciences*: "The 134 items in Jakobson's bibliography that were published between 1920 and 1939 include studies on all the major topics that have occupied Jakobson during his entire career." Only a few scholars display such concentration of scientific dynamism. There exists a theory that this quality is found only among the scholars of a certain number of disciplines, for example mathematicians. No matter what the case, a phenomenon of this sort always appears unusual: there is neither "apprenticeship" nor "growth." Everything is given from the start, as if there were a program for life. Gogol is an analogous example among writers. But let us return to the artistic context of the research of this scholar.

At the beginning of our dialogues, Roman Jakobson said, "I grew up among painters." He traced his connections to Malevich and to their joint scientifico-artistic plans. I would like to add a few more facts about the

knowledge that the young scholar gained by being sur-
rounded from an early age by painters and poets. While
still an adolescent, well before his meetings with Malevich, Roman Jakobson formed friendships with two
young men of his own age, both partisans of pictorial
search: Sergej Maksimovich Bajdin (1894–1920), one of
the first abstract painters in Moscow, and Isaak L'vovich
Kan (1895–1944), who later became a constructivist ar-
chitect. As early as 1911–1912 Jakobson became friends
with Adolf Mil'man, a landscape painter of the Derain
style. In fact, it was Mil'man, an active member of the
"Knave of Hearts" group, who brought him to see the
collection belonging to Shchukin, one of the Moscow mil-
lionaires at the beginning of the century who were en-
thusiasts of French avant-garde painting.

Jakobson's letter to M. V. Matjushin (1861–1934), dating
from the beginning of 1915, perfectly characterizes the
interests, friendships, and activities of those years. The
letter informs us that Jakobson "had returned the paintings to Malevich and had become closer acquainted with
him," and that he had "taken the *Nebesnye verbljužata*
[*Little Heavenly Camels*, a posthumous book by the avant-
garde poetess Elena Guro (1877–1913)] to the editors of
the newspaper *Russkie vedomosti*." And further:

I will send you the photographs of the paintings of Bajdin
later. . . . As for Khlebnikov, the prophecy was fully realized: the Germans sank the *Formidable* on the twentieth. And then, for some reason, I did not have time in
Petersburg to convey one idea to you: it seems to me that
we are not with Don Quixote, we are with the peasants
and hooligans who strike him. For he is a romantic, a
genuflector; he glorifies the past, the fraud that raises us.
Are we not struggling with a knight? What is happening
with Kruchenykh? For some reason he has not answered

my letter. . . . I don't know if Malevich had the time to write to you—it seemed to us that the publication of a collection would be most timely, even in a minimum of copies. It would make a mockery of those gravediggers of innovations. . . .

He then describes the plan for the collection. Almost all of the painters and poets referred to in this letter appear in the text of our dialogues. Some remarks require explanation. As for Khlebnikov, the letter refers to a prophecy he had made based on a mathematical calculation of world events. The reflection on Don Quixote alludes to conversations on the music of Matjushin, which had been inspired, on the one hand, by Don Quixote himself, and, on the other, by a piece written by Matjushin's wife Elena Guro, a poetess and artist close to the Futurists, who had herself been inspired by the life of this errant knight, "that eternal child." The addressee of the letter, Mikhail Vasil'evich Matjushin, was one of the most interesting and impassioned personalities in the domain of avant-garde art, and in avant-garde science and thought in general. A composer, musicologist, painter, and sculptor all at once, he also authored an extremely interesting study on the new perception of space, "Opyt xudožnika novoj mery" ("An artist's experience of the new dimension"). In this work, as in his pedagogical experiments, he examined the problem of the "fourth dimension" which interested the avant-garde at that time, enlivened as they were by the discussions of the physicists.

In 1913, Roman Jakobson became personally acquainted with the eminent painters Mikhail Larionov (1881–1964) and Natal'ja Goncharova (1881–1962). He later saw them several times in Paris, up until their deaths. He still has two abstract drawings by Larionov as a souvenir of these encounters. One of the drawings is inscribed with the dedication, "To Professor Jakobson—An illustration for the poem 'Solnce' ('Sun') by V. V. Majakovskij." The personal acquaintance and subsequent friendship between the linguist Jakobson, fascinated by poetic experimentation, and the poet Vladimir Majakovskij, who was soon to become an enthusiast of a linguistic approach to poetry, to the point of frequenting the Moscow Linguistic Circle and actively participating in its discussions, dates from the time of the poet's meetings with Elsa Triolet (1896–1971) in Moscow and with Osip Brik in Petersburg. One of Majakovskij's interventions is described in Jakobson's "Linguistics and Poetics." One day, when the discussion was turning around the *epitheta ornantia*, Majakovskij declared that to him, any adjective that entered verse automatically became a poetic epithet, even the terms "great" and "little" in such Moscow street names as "Great Presnja" and "Little Presnja."

Roman Jakobson devoted a considerable part of his book *O češskom stixe . . . (On Czech Verse . . .)* to Majakovskij's principles of versification. There he explained for the first time the substance of their global innovation. The readings of Majakovskij's poems that Jakobson recorded at Harvard and in Moscow clearly demonstrate the originality of the poet's own intonations, as well as his "isolated" epithets, which were literally "taken out of brackets"—one would think it a vestige of the old conversation about Great and Little Presnja. Jakobson evoked this in a letter that he sent to me in Warsaw in 1958: "Volodja used to say, 'When one knows the intonation of a poet, the verse resonates completely differently. Here is my living verse, running from me to you, and from you farther on.' " In similar fashion, those who had known Khlebnikov used to say that Roman Jakobson remained faithful to the poet's own voice in interpreting his verse. The recording Jakobson made in 1956 at the Majakovskij Museum in Moscow was played back at a commemorative evening for Khlebnikov. As proof of Jakobson's passion for Majakovskij, we could cite his attempts at translating the poet's verse, particularly his masterful translation into French of the first part of the poem "Oblako v štanax" ("A Cloud in Trousers"). He read his text in January of 1917 to Brik, his wife Lili (1891–1980), and Majakovskij, who all praised its virtuosity. The following year, amid his preoccupation with ancient Slavic poetry, Jakobson translated Majakovskij's facetious poem "Ničego ne ponimajut" ("They Understand Nothing"), which had appeared in the Futurist almanac *Rykajuščij Parnas* ("Roaring Parnassus") in 1914, into Old Church Slavonic and in the metrical system of the didactic poetry of the ninth century.

All of Majakovskij's readers are acquainted with "Romka Jakobson," the diminutive of "Roman" that the poet used in his popular poem, "Tovariščju Nette—paroxodu i čeloveku" ("To Comrade Nette—Steamship and Man," 1926):

Do you remember, Nette—
    the times when, as a man,
you drank tea with me
    in the diplomatic compartment?
You were dawdling,
    and the dormice began to snore

One eye
   crossing at the wax seal
   you chatted all night of Romka Jakobson . . .

Nette was a Soviet diplomatic courier, and had been devoted to poetry from an early age. Upon his return to Moscow from Prague at the end of 1920, Nette gave Majakovskij a letter from Roman Jakobson that recommended the bearer of the message to him. Majakovskij related that, from then on, he often shared Nette's compartment when travelling outside Russia, and that they would speak of their "common friend." Majakovskij composed the poem in question after Nette died in Latvia while "shooting at bandits who had attacked him."

Majkovskij's rhymed dedications are typical of him: "Tebe Romka, xvali gromko" ("To you, Romka, praise me loudly") in the volume of his work published in 1919; "Milyj Romik! dlja novyx xvalenij novyj tomik" ("Dear Roman, praise me anew for a new small work") in the little volume *Majakovskij dlja golosa* (*Majakovskij for Voice*), which appeared in Berlin in June 1923.

Roman Jakobson often referred to his memories of Majakovskij, and he told me once that the poet "did not like what the English call 'small talk,' which was only gossip for him. In general, he would either gamble or write verse." This recollection enables us to understand all that Majakovskij wrote in his works, which are fundamentally "anti-quotidian." He had a morbid aversion to the banality of the everyday, to that odious cliché conveyed in the untranslatable Russian term *byt*.

In October of 1977, a text by Boris Arvatov (1896–1940) was published for the first time in the Paris collection, *Change*. Arvatov, a collaborator with Majakovskij on *Lef*

(*Left-Front*), wrote the piece shortly after the poet's death. In it, Arvatov attempted to define the personality of the dead poet in psychoanalytic terms, a definition that substantially coincides with Roman Jakobson's formulation. Majakovskij's contemporaries had not recognized his true character. Established literary critics always gloss over the most important particularities of his poetry, as Jakobson discovered and noted in an article in 1930. Two of his fundamental works devoted to Majakovskij develop the idea of an alternation in the poet's work between lyrical cycles and waves of "civil" poetry. By his own admission, Majakovskij had returned to the latter in the name of a duty of which he was profoundly aware: "I subjugated myself, putting my foot on the throat of my own song."

As strange as it may seem, Roman Jakobson was the only one who, after the poet's death, revealed the tragic character of Majakovskij's lyrics, with their myth of the martyr-poet who is ultimately condemned to a self-willed fate. Majakovskij's prophecy escaped his contemporaries. "They didn't believe it, they thought they were chimeras"—so Boris Pasternak expressed it in his verse on the death of the poet. In his obituary essay of 1930, *O pokolenii, rastrativšem svoix poètov* (*On the Generation that Squandered its Poets*), Jakobson exposed for the first time, in all its grandeur, the powerful figure of the poet who, during his brief lifetime, struggled courageously against the paralyzing ties of time and space, who attempted to overcome death, to acquire immortality for the future of all humanity. Roman Jakobson showed us in his article the true face of Majakovskij, the face of all Russian Futurism, with its Promethian utopia of a sortie into the cosmos and a victory over the cosmic forces.

   This moving obituary, which was described by Jakobson's close friend Petr Grigor'evich Bogatyrev as the most
powerful piece that Jakobson had ever written or could
ever have written, is filled with the living memory of
Majakovskij. Here is its most characteristic passage:

When in the spring of 1920 I returned to Moscow, which
was tightly blockaded, I brought with me recent books
and information about scientific developments in the
West. Majakovskij made me repeat several times my
somewhat confused remarks on the general theory of
relativity, and about the growing interest in that concept
in Western Europe. The idea of the liberation of energy,
the problem of the time dimension, and the idea that
movement at the speed of light may actually be a reverse
movement in time—all of these things fascinated
Majakovskij. I'd seldom seen him so interested and attentive. "Don't you think," he suddenly asked, "that we'll
at last achieve immortality?" I was astonished, and I
mumbled a skeptical comment. He thrust his jaw forward
with that hypnotic insistence so familiar to anyone who
knew Majakovskij well: "I'm absolutely convinced," he
said, "that one day there will be no more death. And the
dead will be raised from the dead. I've got to find some
scientist who'll give me a precise account of what's in
Einstein's books. It's out of the question that I shouldn't
understand it. I'll see to it that the scientist receives an
academician's ration."

One could not express better the exaltation of the quest
of that time, and all the interests of the generation and
the environment in which Jakobson grew up and lived.
   In our dialogues, mention has been made of that other
influential figure, the supraconscious poet Aleksej Eliseevich Kruchenykh. Roman Jakobson made his acquaintance, along with Khlebnikov's, before he entered
the university. He saw him often and carried on an extended correspondence with him. The young disciple of

linguistics remained a fervent Futurist, and signed his supraconscious verse with the pseudonym R. Aljagrov. It was with this pseudonym that the seventeen-year-old Jakobson signed in 1914 an extant letter to Kruchenykh in which he gives the latest literary news of Moscow: "The daily papers, the magazines, the shop windows are invaded by articles on Futurism, and some seem to be taking it seriously." A list of conferences on Futurism is followed by an appreciation of the new poetry of the Futurists, an appreciation that, marked with all the ardor typical of the youngest and most militant activists of art, is near in both spirit and style to the Futurist manifestos:

For until now, poetry has been a glass-blower, and just like the light of the sun passing through these lenses, the romanticized demonism has in its transparency given it a picturesque aspect. But now the victory over the sun [an allusion to Kruchenykh's play of the same name, performed in Petersburg in 1913] and the F-ray (borrowed from your writings) have shattered the glass, and out of the splinters . . . we are creating patterns in the name of liberation. Out of this demonism, this zero, we can create any kind of conventionality, and in its intensity, its power, lies the guarantee of aristocratism in poetry.

This letter, which resembles a recording of theoretical reflections, expresses both the Futurist theory of the "self-sufficient word" (*samovitoe slovo*), and the composition of the whole "out of the splinters" and of "any conventionality out of the zero." The latter is an idea that resonates with those of Khlebnikov when he speaks of the principal "units of construction" of the new genre, the suprastory (*sverxpovest'*). In his introduction to the poem-drama *Zangezi* of 1922, Khlebnikov wrote that, unlike the simple narrative that is constructed out of words, the "suprastory or meta-story [*zapovest'*] is constructed from autonomous fragments, each with its own god, its own faith, and its own status. . . . The unit of construction, the building block of the suprastory, is itself a story of the first order. It resembles a statue made of many-colored blocks of different natures. . . . It is carved out of the polychromatic blocks of the word, of different constructions."

According to Jakobson, the meditations in which Khlebnikov engaged later in his life "sometimes mirrored our conversations on the subject of the word in poetry." The first time he read Khlebnikov's poems in 1912, Jakobson saw in him the greatest poet of our era. Angelo Maria Ripellino (1922—1979), a subtle judge of literary art, agreed with this estimation in his book *Poesie di Chlebnikov* (Turin, 1968). "Jakobson published a study on me," Khlebnikov announced to his mother in April 1922, in his last letter to her.

Roman Jakobson's letters to Khlebnikov have for the most part been preserved in the archives of N. I. Khardzhiev (1903–), the great connoisseur of the Russian and European avant-garde. The content of one of these letters, as Khardzhiev states in his "Poèzija i živopis'," in *K istorii russkogo avangarda* ("Poetry and Painting," in *Towards a History of the Russian Avant-Garde*, Stockholm, 1976), is close, both in time (1914) and in its theme, to his letter to Kruchenykh:

You recall, Viktor Vladimirovich, that you once said our alphabet was too poor for poetry, and you asked how one could avoid ending up at an impasse with our verse based on letters. I am ever more convinced that you were wrong. I have recently found a curious novelty, so I am writing to you about it. This novelty is braided letters—an analogy to musical chords, to a certain extent. One thus comes to a simultaneity of two or more letters, and to a diversity of graphic combinations establishing different relations between letters as well. This idea enriches verse and opens up new paths. . . . When I asked you what you had come up with, you answered: the number. You know, Viktor Vladimirovich, it seems to me that poems made of numbers are possible. The number is a double-edged sword—it is extremely concrete and extremely abstract, arbitrary and fatally precise, logical and absurd, limited and infinite. . . . Numbers are familiar to you, and even if you believe that numerical poetry is a sharp paradox, albeit inadmissible, try, if you will, to give me a brief sample of this sort of verse.

As Khardzhiev remarks, "Jakobson's letter itself contains examples of his unpronounceable 'literal' verse." In the letter to Kruchenykh, Aljagrov undertakes an analogous experiment, the creation of verse made up of vowels and other forms of "graphic" poetry: "You ask me," he writes, "where I could have seen verse made of vowels. The magical formulas of the gnostics are an interesting example of this. As you recall, you were saying that any category of letters in direct or inverse order constitutes poetry, and you called that a demonic or underground standpoint."

One can find the same communion of thought between the young Jakobson and the painter Malevich. In the course of our dialogues, we mentioned a letter from Malevich to Matjushin (1916) in which the author establishes an analogy between abstract, particularly Suprematist, painting and supraconscious poetry, which, as Jakobson puts it, "coincides in many respects with our conversations of that time." Let us cite the most characteristic of Malevich's reflections contained in this letter:

When we had arrived at the idea of sound, we obtained note-letters which expressed phonic masses. Perhaps in the composition of these phonic masses (former words) one can find a new path. Thus we tear the letter from its line, its singular direction, and we give it the possibility of free movement. (Lines suit only the world of bureaucracy and domestic correspondence.) Consequently, we come to . . . the distribution of a lot of letter-sounds in space, just like Suprematism in painting. These masses will be suspended in space and will procure for our consciousness the possibility of penetrating even farther from Earth.

Malevich's letter coincides with the very style of Jakobson's letters. These messages all have the character of a free notation of thoughts on art, which is apparent even in their graphical form: the long text is broken down into fragments separated not by paragraphs but by asterisks. Roman Jakobson said that his letters to Kruchenykh and Khlebnikov made use of ideas he had progressively jotted down after slow walks around the Polytechnic Museum of Moscow in the evenings after school. During these walks he would reflect upon poetry and poetic language, and upon returning home he would write his thoughts in little black notebooks. This sort of correspondence, which aimed at a veritable intellectual exchange, is characteristic of that period, and of the men of the Russian avant-garde in particular.

Jakobson devotes part of his letter to Kruchenykh to a description of his own poetry:

I am responding to your recent request, Aleksej Eliseevich, and am sending you a poem which I wrote three weeks ago which is, in a certain sense, verbal. The word is not sufficient unto itself: it dies of a broken heart in its aspiration to laconism and arhythmy. All the words in it are of the masculine gender, as you requested. With me, the word is not self-sufficient, for the self-sufficient word supposes certain statics on the part of the author, which, however, are not fully realizable—these are elementary truths.

As one can see, the young partisan of Futurism attempts to surpass Kruchenykh himself, in both theory and application, through his audacious experiments.

Kruchenykh published a few texts that Jakobson sent him in 1914—experiments in supraconscious poetry with a fixation on an unusual combination of consonants—in the almost unobtainable collection of 1916, *Zaumnaja gniga* (*Supraconscious Book*). The volume contained verse by Kruchenykh and Aljagrov, and color engravings by the painter Ol'ga Rozanova. Some of the experiments undertaken at that time by Aljagrov were also published in Kruchenykh's pamphlet, *Zaumniki* (1922).

Jakobson met Kruchenykh again much later, in 1956, when he began to attend various international scientific congresses in Moscow. At that time, Kruchenykh was living in a communal apartment across from the main post office. He occupied a tiny room that was virtually impossible to enter, crammed as it was from floor to ceiling with books and extremely valuable manuscripts, all of which were covered with a layer of dust. The master of the house received his guests either in the kitchen or in a room lent to him for the occasion by neighbors. Aleksej Eliseevich would celebrate each visit of his old friend and collaborator in his own way: first he would offer to his guests the wine which they themselves had brought, and then cut his own wine with boiling water. During one of these vists, he offered Jakobson an extremely rare book: the last issue of *Neizdannyj Xlebnikov* (*Unpublished Khlebnikov*). Wearing a curious bathrobe, with an even stranger white muffler tied around his neck and his feet only in worn-out bedroom slippers, Kruchenykh was nevertheless extremely alert and full of truly Futurist ideas. In the course of these serious but animated conversations, he would ask us little literary riddles, which, of course, he would solve himself. I recall two of them. The first was, "What was the profession of Blok's *Neznakomka* [*Unknown Lady*]?" Answer: fashion model. The second: "What was the theme of the Gogolian novelette 'Vij'?" Answer: a tournament of supraconscious poets. Aleksej Eliseevich had a speech "defect," a "stuttered" language (*zatrudnennaja reč'*), a lisp, which he affected on purpose purely as a matter of Futurist principles. In fact, this "speech defect" disappeared completely whenever Kruchenykh read verse aloud. And he declaimed marvelously. He would dramatize his poem "Vesna s dvumja priglašenijami" ("A spring with two invitations") with all sorts of sound effects: he would stamp his foot or strike rhythmic blows with the chair he was holding onto during the recitation. The back of the chair would serve him sometimes as a tribunal bannister, sometimes as an instrument for his sound effects, sometimes as protection against the public. . . . The last time we heard him, in about 1967, he was reading with a somewhat less booming voice but still quite well, and with a particularly bizarre sound device: "The chandelier! It has fallen on the bald head of the old nobleman!" He would scream out the first word while covering his mouth with his hand in order to direct his voice toward the ceiling, toward a real chandelier that would begin to tremble and resonate. Between these two old friends, there was never any question of the "past" or of recollections. One would have thought that they had just seen each other the day before from the way they always discussed current topics, especially books and poetry. In the main, it was Kruchenykh who spoke or recited his poems.

From the moment of his arrival in Czechoslovakia in 1920, Roman Jakobson was very closely connected with poets and artists. The experiences of his youth were being repeated, or rather were simply continuing. The first Czech poet whom he met and with whom he became friends was Stanislav Kostka Neumann (1875–1947). Neumann published Jakobson's first Czech paper, "On Realism in Art," in one of his two militant magazines, and presented in the other the Czech translation of the introductory chapter to Jakobson's research on Khlebnikov. Still, Jakobson felt infinitely more affinity towards the ideas and experiments of Prague's youngest writers and painters, and became particularly close to the poets Vítězslav Nezval and Jaroslav Seifert (1901–), the prose writer Vladislav Vančura, and the theoretician Karel Teige (1900–1951). Teige had been one of the founders of a union known under the name "Devětsil," to which Jakobson would soon be elected as a member.

I have never heard anyone read poetry aloud as remarkably as Roman Jakobson read the poems of Nezval. He always placed the works of Nezval and Seifert among the highest accomplishments of the literature of our century. In his notes of the time, published among his memoirs (1959), Nezval wrote the following:

In Roman Jakobson I found a friend for life. We always saw eye to eye on matters of poetry. He had been the friend of Majakovskij, of Pasternak, of the Russian Futurists, and his experiences always interested us. He defended us against the reactionaries of art, and, in our disputes with him, he would always make his points as a polemicist without peer! He had the rare gift of being able to gather around a table people whom no one else could have assembled under one roof. . . . Vladislav Vančura loved him for his understanding of the work of the writer on the word and of the writer's decisive role.

Jakobson greatly appreciated Vančura, man and writer, and always admired the novelty of his prose. Vančura perished heroically during the German occupation, and his widow devotes one chapter of her memoirs (Prague, 1967)—a moving book, full of talent—to the friendship between her husband and Jakobson:

Among Vančura's friends, the individuals of the Linguistic Circle, and particularly Jakobson, Mukařovský, [Bohuslav] Havránek [1893–1978], and Bogatyrev, formed a special group. Their friendship was based on actively shared interests, mutual admiration, and esteem; this friendship, especially in the case of Jakobson and Mukařovský, extended even to their families. Roman Jakobson, Russian by origin, was one of the most gifted Slavists and Bohemists, an unusual man both in appearance and in nature. A powerful man, with a rather large head, thick blond hair, and the face of a Roman god, he squinted in one eye. But he was not one to be bothered by such a troublesome defect. He overflowed with vitality, spoke with passion, and gestured with spirit. . . . Vladislav felt happy among such friends—he was drawn to Jakobson's ardor and élan, he loved the debates with Mukařovský, who never departed from his academic seriousness.

Among the Slovaks, two eminent militants of the cultural avant-garde became particularly close to Roman Jakobson: the poet Ladislav Novomeský (1904–1976) and the political activist Vladimir Clementis (1902–1952). On the occasion of Jakobson's seventieth birthday, Novomeský launched the publication of the review *Slovenská literatura* with an article entitled "S avangardom i v avangarde" ("With the Avant-Garde and Within the Avant-Garde"):

Roman Jakobson—whether one likes it or not—has become an indispensable link in the chain of the artistic and scientific avant-garde of the Czechs and the Slovaks. He holds a well-deserved place in the history of our culture, and his name should not and cannot be omitted from it. . . . He is so well-grounded in the problems of our science and our art that it is often difficult for us to tell whether he is a Russian scholar who has spent the years of his youth in Czechoslovakia or a Czech scholar whom the whirlwind of Nazism carried far off from us to Harvard.

Of this sojourn in Czechoslovakia there remains one significant document, the brochure "To Roman Jakobson, With Our Greetings and Gratitude." This was published in 1939 by the students of the University of Brno when Jakobson was forced to leave his professorial chair because of pressure from Berlin. This work once again illustrates the connection between science and poetry that we have termed "feedback." Arne Novák (1880–1939), rector of the University of Brno and a celebrated historian of Czech literature, as well as an intimate friend of Jakobson's, devoted an article in this brochure to him entitled, "The Creative Expert on Old Czech Poetry." The article ends as follows: 'If God wills it, we will soon see Jakobson again, a professor where he truly belongs. For science and culture could not exist if those who are not called were always to choose those who are called." The brochure opens with one of Nezval's couplets: "More than any other, Roman, you respond to my hidden well-springs," and it ends with a letter from the poet to Jakobson followed by the line "Roman, thank you for everything!" There is in these lines an expression of deep gratitude for the impulses to "turn documents into verses," and "to convert the entire world to rhyme, just as the rich man turns it into revenue." As Jaroslav Seifert said in his memoirs, "It falls to experts to evaluate Jakobson's work for us. It will be a beautiful and rich chapter. My part is to recollect all that which was elusive but still beautiful." Such was the movement that united the avant-garde of poetry and science.

Upon his arrival in New York in 1941, Jakobson found there a group of Polish poets who had fled occupied War- saw: Julian Tuwim, Józef Wittlin (1896–1976), and Kazimierz Wierzyński (1894–1969). Jakobson had already formed a friendship with Tuwim in Prague. He admired Tuwim's translations of Russian poetry and had often discussed with him in their meetings and correspondence the problems of translating poetry. Their animated con- versations continued in New York, developing into a dis- cussion about different problems in Polish and Russian literary art, about the poem "Flowers of Poland," which Tuwim was working on at the time, and about the theory of translation—in particularly in regard to the new version of *Slovo o polku Igoreve* (*The Igor Tale*), which Tuwim had rendered in Polish verse. During the sixties, Jakobson became close friends with Wierzyński, greatly appreci- ating his poems and working to analyze them. He always quoted, in fact, the great Polish linguist K. Nitsch (1874–1958), who said that the innovative spirit of the Polish poetic tradition culminated in Wierzyński's poetry. The poet discussed poetry and language with Jakobson. He followed the linguist's articles, and he once wrote to me in a somewhat joking manner, "I must spend my nights studying in order not to be completely left behind by his linguistic eccentricities. He believes that he observes some success in me in this regard. . . ."

Among the research interests that Jakobson shared with non-Slavic poets on questions of literary art, one should cite the fascinating attempt at direct collaboration with the great Mexican poet Octavio Paz on the grammatical and phonic analysis of the latter's poetry. Jakobson also knew the eminent Brazilian poet and critic Haroldo de Campos, a master of poetic translation, with whom he carried on a lively exchange of observations and conclusions. This experience is reflected in a published letter, "To Haroldo de Campos on the poetic texture of Martin Codax." We should also mention the close ties between Jakobson and Louis Aragon, the author of the linguistic novel *Blanche ou l'oubli*.

The system of feedback in the relations between the linguist and the world's avant-garde poets is not simply an exchange of thought and impulses. It is much more subtle, and its sources lie at the depths of the scientific method and of literary art. Referring to his collaboration with Khlebnikov in 1919 on the preparation of his poems for publication, Jakobson offers the following comment: "It would be difficult to find a poet who could combine more thoroughly, both in principle and in poetic creation, the phonic structure with the semantic plane. I came to apply linguistic methods to the phonic analysis of texture in Khlebnikov. Moreover, the new light that this poet's original work shed on sounds led me despite myself to put into question the traditional conception of phonic material in linguistics and to submit it to a fundamental revision."

One can, *mutatis mutandis*, say the same of all the points of tangency between the linguist and world poetry.

Jakobson came to this realization for the first time in 1923, while working on *O česskom stixe . . . (On Czech Verse . . .)*. He continued on to a concrete analysis of poetic material in several languages, and succeeded in distinguishing clearly two categories of phonic phenomena in language: phonic phenomena that signify and those that do not signify. This was particularly clear from the fact that phonic elements of the first category were of primary importance to verse. He thus made poetry influence directly the explanation and development of phonological theory, and established a direct link between this analysis and linguistics as a science. Similarly, while editing the translations of Pushkin into Czech in Prague, the scholar came up against the question of grammatical categories, their obligatory character, and the fact that they were untranslatable, a problem which was also taken up in the work of Edward Sapir. Jakobson acquired a particular sensitivity to questions of poetic semantics throughout the years when he observed the experiments of avant-garde poets in the areas of phonology, morphology, and syntax, and these experiments no doubt strengthened similar tendencies in his own nature.

From the beginning, Roman Jakobson has always abided by the following principle: control the results of research on any given material by applying them to other material. He constantly asked himself what an observed phenomenon corresponded to in another domain of art. Thus he moved from dialectology and folklore to painting, film and journalism. In Czechoslovakia, he worked on producing a film and studied other forms of montage as well, especially literary montage, which interested a number of avant-garde scholars at that time. Roman Jakobson's colleagues in the OPOJAZ wrote a good deal about these matters. He himself published some attempts at literary montage in the Czech press during the thirties: for example, his "Perpetual Motion of the Pendulum" (1934), which consists of a mixture of extracts from the book by Alexander Herzen (1812–1870) on the events of 1848 adapted to the international situation of 1934. Four years later, he published "Russian Sorties into the Future," in which he assembled heterogeneous and discontinuous conjectures on revolution selected from classic prose and poetry "from Radishchev to Dostoevskij and Tolstoj, on up to the Futurist poets, who had even given a date for the revolution they predicted . . ." From *We and They* (1931), Savich and Ehrenburg's extensive survey of Russian literary testimonies and judgments of France and the French, Jakobson was able to draw a succinct montage sketching out the "Russian myth of France" in his essay by that title published in 1938 in the review *Slavische Rundschau.*

Even these "asides" reveal the basic drive of Jakobson's works, his passion for researching the constants among countless variables, be they the invariants within a single linguistic system, universal invariants, or even the invariants of different disciplines compared. All of this research issues from the Heraclitean premise that variation is the universal invariant.

The Russian linguist Igor' Mel'chuk, who collaborated on the large volume *Echoes of his Scholarship* published in honor of Roman Jakobson's eightieth birthday, showed a keen appreciation of Jakobson's general contribution to science in the world. On the subject of the invariants that Jakobson had discovered throughout his interdisciplinary studies and to which he devoted increasing attention, Mel'chuk wrote:

It would be difficult to find a linguist in our day who examined in such an intense and fundamental way the connections between linguistics and the other sciences: linguistics and poetics, linguistics and musicology, linguistics and anthropology, linguistics and information theory, linguistics and the theory of translation, linguistics and mathematics, linguistics and psychology, linguistics and semiotics—and the list goes on. This is what Roman Jakobson devoted a constant and active attention to.

Intrepid research, totally without scientific conformism—an absence that did not fail to disconcert many a contemporary—this is the trait that characterizes the entire *oeuvre* of Roman Jakobson.

Krystyna Pomorska

BIBLIOGRAPHY

Jakobson, Roman
Selected Writings. Hawthorne, New York: Mouton.
  I. *Phonological Studies,* 1971
 II: *Word and Language,* 1971
III: *Poetry of Grammar and Grammar of Poetry,* 1980
IV: *Slavic Epic Studies,* 1966
 V: *On Verse, Its Masters and Explorers,* 1978
VI: *Early Slavic Paths and Crossroads,* 1982

Jakobson, Roman,
1978. *Six Lectures on Sound and Meaning.* Cambridge, Massachusetts: MIT Press.

Jakobson, Roman, and Linda R. Waugh
1979. *The Sound Shape of Language.* Bloomington, Indiana: Indiana University Press.

Jakobson, Roman
1980. *The Framework of Language.* Ann Arbor, Michigan: Michigan Slavic Publications.

Jakobson, Roman
1980. *Brain and Language.* Columbus, Ohio: Slavica Publishers.

Armstrong, Daniel, and C. H. van Schooneveld, eds.
1977. *Roman Jakobson—Echoes of His Scholarship.* Bloomington, Indiana: P. de Ridder.

Holenstein, Elmar
1974. *Roman Jakobson's Approach to Language,* Bloomington, Indiana: Indiana University Press.

Hrushovski, Benjamin, ed.
1980. *Roman Jakobson—Language and Literature. Poetics Today* 2, No. la.

Koch, Walter A., ed.
1982. *Semiogenesis: Essays on the Analysis of the Genesis of Language, Art, and Literature,* Vol. I (Dedicated to Roman Jakobson). Germany: Peter Lang.

van Schooneveld, C. H.
1971. *Roman Jakobson—A Bibliography of His Writings.* Hawthorne, New York: Mouton.

Waugh, Linda R.
1976. *Roman Jakobson's Science of Language.* Bloomington, Indiana: P. de Ridder.